SCOTTISH HISTORY

HarperCollins Publishers
Westerhill Road
Bishopbriggs
Glasgow
G64 2QT

First Edition 2014
Second Edition 2017

Reprint 10 9 8 7 6 5 4 3 2 1 0

© HarperCollins Publishers 2017

ISBN 978-0-00-825110-9

Collins® is a registered trademark
of HarperCollins Publishers
Limited

www.collins.co.uk

A catalogue record for this book is
available from the British Library

Author: John Abernethy

Typeset by Davidson Publishing
Solutions

Printed and bound in China by
RR Donnelley APS Co Ltd

Contents

Introduction   4

Scottish History   9

Conclusion   214

Index   216

Introduction

Compiling the *Little Book of Scottish History* has been a wonderful challenge. With thousands of years of history as source material there is an extraordinary wealth of information and facts to call on, and so many famous – and not so famous – lives whose stories deserve to be told, from Neolithic times through to the digital age of the 21st century.

With the *Little Book of Scottish History* we have attempted to give as broad an overview as possible. Yes, we cover the more familiar topics of William Wallace, Robert the Bruce, Mary, Queen of Scots, Robert Burns, the battles of Bannockburn and Culloden, the Highland clans, and the historic role of Edinburgh, the capital of Scotland. However, we also recognize the equally important events that shaped Scotland into the country it is today: a nation that was forged first by the union of the Picts and Gaelic-speaking incomers from Ireland, and grew over time to incorporate the Lowland kingdoms of Lothian and Strathclyde, and the formerly Scandinavian-ruled Hebrides and Northern Isles. In doing so we trace the development of a nation and people that were given the name 'Caledonia' by the Romans, then 'Alba' by the Gaels, before settling on 'Scotland', the land of the Scots.

The kingdom of Scotland endured for 700 years through adversity, conflict, and seemingly insurmountable odds until the Union of Crowns with England in 1603 and the Union of Parliaments in 1707. However, even after Union, the Scottish people have retained their independent culture, heritage, and spirit into the modern age, both at home and abroad. After 1707 itinerant Scots travelled the globe in ever greater numbers, taking their language, their religion, and their history with them to their new homes. Over time this Scottish history, as history always does, became interwoven with mythology and legend to create a rich and colourful tapestry, so wherever possible we have tried to differentiate the fact from the myth – or explain why the legend became so important.

By giving due recognition to the history of Scotland and the Scots after 1707, we will also attempt to bring the story up to date. Scots played a pivotal role in the Enlightenment, the Industrial Revolution, and the British Empire. In the process they not only built modern Scotland, but also an extraordinary amount of the modern world, from the telephone to television, and from radio waves to penicillin. Scotland's ongoing scientific, industrial, and medical legacy is another chapter of the story that we will investigate, alongside such iconic aspects of the nation's culture as tartan, whisky, and golf. For it is only by examining all elements of Scotland and the Scots that we gain a true picture of the country and its people.

History matters, for it tells us who we are, how we got here, and why the world is the way it is. And for a country such as Scotland, where the question of national identity can have many different and sometimes contradictory answers, history matters more than for most. The *Little Book of Scottish History* is our attempt to provide a concise summary of over 2000 years of Scottish history. We hope that it answers and explains all the questions you ever wanted to ask, as well as a few that you never even thought to. We also hope you enjoy our *Little Book of Scottish History* as an informative and entertaining introduction to a subject that has never had such a large global audience. For that is the most wonderful thing about history: there are always more stories to be told.

About the author

John Abernethy was born in Shetland and today resides in Edinburgh. He has worked for most of his life in bookselling, publishing, and tourism, but his passion has always been history. John had his first work published in 2005, and has subsequently written extensively on many aspects of Scottish history, from etymology to sport, but has also written books for children, collaborated with renowned singer and actress, Barbara Dickson, and recently appeared on *Mastermind*.

SCOTTISH HISTORY

Prehistoric Scotland

Located on the western fringes of the European continent, Scotland was one of the last regions to be inhabited after the end of the last Ice Age. The first humans arrived over 9,000 years ago, around 7,000 BC, and were nomadic hunters and gatherers, but settled as farmers. The oldest surviving evidence of their Neolithic society is found at the village of Skara Brae in Orkney, which dates back 5,000 years to around 3,000 BC. Orkney is a treasure trove of reminders of prehistoric Scotland, with Skara Brae and the magnificent burial tomb of Maes Howe as its centrepiece. Further west, on the Hebridean island of Lewis, stands the equally impressive stone circle of Calanais (Callanish), which also dates back to the third millennium BC. It is highly probable that there are many other equally important artefacts of the first natives buried deep beneath the peat and earth of the islands of Scotland, but even from what has been found so far, we can tell that a sophisticated culture and widespread trading routes had been established thousands of years before the more recent reputation of the Scots as an ingenious and exceedingly well-travelled people.

The Romans

The first surviving record of the people who lived in the land that we now know as Scotland came in AD 79 when the all-conquering Romans arrived in Scotland under the general Agricola. In AD 84 Agricola defeated the Celtic tribes who lived in eastern and northern Scotland in a mighty battle in the Cairngorms – although we only have the Romans' word for how glorious this victory actually was. During the next century the Romans reinforced their position in their most northerly territory by building forts, garrisons, and, in AD 143, the Antonine Wall, which stretched from the River Forth in the east to the River Clyde in the west. The Romans gave the name 'Caledonia' to what is now Scotland. However, whether through choice or through their inability to subdue the resistance of the local tribes they encountered, the Romans never succeeded in making Caledonia anything more than a military outpost. In AD 180 the Romans left Caledonia and retreated southwards to Hadrian's Wall, in what is now the north of England, never to return. The forts and the Antonine Wall were abandoned, and so ended the first attempt of many to unite the island of Britain under the rule of one empire.

The Picts

It was the Romans who gave the Celts who lived in Scotland the name of 'Picts', deriving from the Latin 'Picti', meaning 'painted ones', on account of the body paint they wore in battle. And it was the Romans, with their departure from Caledonia, who gave credence to the Picts' historical reputation as a warrior people that even the world's greatest empire could not subdue. Although little is known of the origins of the Picts and their relationship with the other Celtic peoples of Britain and Ireland, the name became associated with the tribes who lived in northern and eastern Scotland. In the centuries that followed the Roman departure in AD 180, the Picts eventually united to establish the kingdom of Pictland. The Picts remained a powerful presence until the 9th century AD, when the kingdoms of the Picts and their principal rivals, the Scots, were first united, but by the following century the Picts had been subsumed into a new Scottish nation and identity, leaving a cultural and political legacy of fierce independence that continued long after their disappearance from history.

The Scots

The people after whom Scotland is named were
Celts from Ireland, who began to arrive in the west
of Scotland in the 4th century AD. It is unclear where
the name 'Scots' came from. Suggestions include
the Latin name 'Scoti', meaning 'raiders', although it
is probable that there are earlier, unknown origins.
These Irish invaders established themselves in what
is now Argyll in their kingdom of Dalriada. When the
kingdoms of the Picts and the Scots became united
in the 9th century AD, it was the Scots who ultimately
proved dominant and it was their culture and Gaelic
language (deriving from 'Gaels', an ancient name
for people of Irish origin) that dominated the new
kingdom of Alba. It was not until the 11th century
that the Lowland kingdoms of Lothian (in 1018) and
Strathclyde (in 1034) finally fell under the rule of
Alba. However, Gaelic never became established in
Lothian and the southeast. Instead it was the Old
English language of Lothian that increasingly gained
precedence in the newly expanded nation, and over
time the Gaelic name of Alba would be replaced by its
English equivalent, Scotland, the land of the Scots.

Christianity

The first record of Christianity in Scotland dates back to AD 397 when St Ninian, a Christian missionary from the north of England, became Bishop of Whithorn in Galloway and built Scotland's first Christian church. While little is known of St Ninian and the first Christians, the site of the first church in Scotland, in Whithorn, which was given the name of *Candida Casa* (or 'the White House'), remained a centre of Christian pilgrimage for the next thousand years.

There also remains a widely held belief that St Ninian's near-contemporary, St Patrick, the patron saint of Ireland, was actually born in Scotland, in Kilpatrick in Dunbartonshire. However, there is no historical evidence to substantiate this claim, and in all probability Patrick, like Ninian, hailed from what is now the north of England. Scotland instead had to look considerably further afield to find a national patron saint to call its own.

St Andrew

The patron saint of Scotland (and also Russia) is
St Andrew, the brother of Peter, and one of the
original Twelve Disciples. According to legend, a relic
pertaining to the apostle, who had been martyred
through crucifixion on an X-shaped cross in Greece
in the 1st century AD, was brought to Scotland at some
time in the 8th century and buried in what became
the historic town of St Andrews in Fife. In the same
century, it was said that, prior to a famous victory by
the Picts over the Northumbrians at Athelstaneford
in East Lothian, a vision appeared in the sky of an
X-shaped white cross against the background of
the blue sky, so beginning the cult of St Andrew as
a symbol of first Pictish and subsequently Scottish
national identity.

The blue-and-white diagonal cross became the Saltire,
the national flag of Scotland, and the feast day of
St Andrew, the 30th of November, became the
national day of Scotland. St Andrew has remained
the patron saint of Scotland to this day, although
tradition also dictates that St Andrew's Day is
celebrated by being almost completely ignored by
most of the Scottish population.

Iona

The small island of Iona, off the coast of the larger
Hebridean island of Mull, has been an important
centre of Christianity in Scotland since the 6th century
AD. In AD 563 the Irish-born St Columba founded
a monastery on Iona and began his mission to
convert Scotland, and particularly the Pictish north,
to Christianity. St Columba died in AD 597 and had
become so influential that for centuries afterwards
the kings of Scotland were buried at his remote
monastery in Iona, and the island remains Scotland's
most iconic spiritual destination to this day. When the
kingdoms of the Picts and the Scots were first united
in AD 843, the relics of St Columba were removed
from Iona and taken to the new royal capital of
Dunkeld in Perthshire in a casket that became known
as the Monymusk Reliquary. The Reliquary became a
symbol of Scottish independence and was carried into
the Battle of Bannockburn in 1314, although today it
can be found in the much more tranquil surroundings
of the Museum of Scotland in Edinburgh.

Alba

Kenneth (or Cináed) mac Alpin is often said to be the first king of Scotland, for around AD 843 he is believed to have become king of both Scots and Picts, so uniting the two nations. In all probability the union between Picts and Scots was a more gradual process involving royal intermarriages and concurrent violent uprisings over a long period of time. However, what made Kenneth mac Alpin a pivotal figure in Scottish history was the Alpin dynasty that would follow. By the 10th century it had established the Gaelic-speaking nation of Alba, and through the Tanistry system of royal succession, by which the crown would pass to the most powerful member of the royal family, rather than the eldest son, it would rule Alba until 1034. The name 'Alba' is derived from the same root as 'Albion', the ancient name for the island of Britain, and it remains the Gaelic name for Scotland to this day.

The Stone of Destiny

According to legend, the Stone of Destiny, the iconic symbol of Scottish nationhood, which today resides in Edinburgh Castle, is the very stone that was both Jacob's pillow in The Book of Genesis and the ancient stone upon which the first Scots kings were crowned in their kingdom of Dalriada from the 5th century AD onwards. In the 9th century, Kenneth mac Alpin transferred the Stone from Dunstaffnage in Argyll to Scone in Perthshire, where until 1297 all kings of first Alba, and then Scotland, were solemnly crowned on the sacred sandstone where Jacob once slept.

In 1297, Edward I of England removed the Stone from Scone to Westminster Abbey in London, where it would remain for 700 years as a seemingly permanent reminder of the supremacy of the English over their Scottish neighbours. The Stone was briefly liberated by enterprising Scottish nationalists in 1950, but was formally returned to Scotland only in 1996. However, whether because of doubts concerning its authenticity, or because of its current residence in Edinburgh rather than Scone, the Stone of Destiny has yet to regain the same national potency that it acquired in exile.

The Vikings

The earliest recorded Viking or Norse attack on Scotland took place in AD 794, and in the 9th century vast areas of Scotland – from Galloway in the south to Shetland in the north – were invaded by these fearsome warriors, who sailed from Norway in their mighty longships. The first Vikings came to raid and plunder, but future generations had more permanent aspirations. While the nation of Scotland was being united as one kingdom in the 11th century, it was the king of Norway, rather than the king of Scotland, who ruled the islands and much of the northern mainland of Scotland. By the 12th century the Norwegians had lost control of their mainland territory, and after losing the Battle of Largs in 1263, they ceded the Hebrides to Scotland in the Treaty of Perth in 1266. However, this would not be the end of Scandinavian influence on the history of Scotland, as Orkney and Shetland remained under first Norwegian and then Danish sovereignty until 1469. The Norse legacy can still be found today in numerous place names throughout the country that stand as a reminder of those formidable and terrifying raiders who eventually settled in their new homeland.

The Northern Isles

From the 9th to the 13th centuries, the Northern Isles of the Orkney and Shetland archipelagos were ruled by the Scandinavian successors to the first Viking raiders. Their leaders were given the title of Earl (or 'Jarl' in Norse) of Orkney, with the most famous being the martyr St Magnus, after whom the 12th-century St Magnus Cathedral in Kirkwall, Orkney, is named. In 1235 the title of Earl passed from Norse to Scottish hands, but sovereignty remained with first the Norwegian and then the Danish crowns, to whom the Scottish Earls continued to swear allegiance. In 1469, Orkney and Shetland were offered to Scotland as a dowry for the marriage of Danish princess Margaret to James III, and they have remained part of Scotland ever since, albeit continuing to speak the Old Norse language of Norn until the 18th century, and in Shetland celebrating their Viking heritage with the annual Up Helly Aa winter fire festival. The acquisition of the Northern Isles completed the map of Scotland that we know today, even if in reality this means Orkney and Shetland are regularly relegated to inserts several hundred miles south of their actual location.

Place names

The place names of Scotland reflect the country's diverse heritage. The majority of Scottish place names are either of Gaelic, Scots, or English origin and roughly follow a Highland–Lowland geographical divide. In Strathclyde and the southwest there are numerous reminders of the old Celtic language of Cumbric (or Brythonic), which comes from the same linguistic family as modern-day Welsh. In the Northern and Western Isles centuries of Scandinavian and Viking rule have left a smorgasbord of place names of Norse origin. Meanwhile, the language of the once-mighty Picts has been all but excluded from the geography of the country they ruled for a millennium.

Under the aegis of the British Empire, when Scots left their homeland to make new lives in the New World, they took their place names with them. Perth in Australia, Calgary in Canada, and Dunedin (the ancient name for Edinburgh) in New Zealand are all named in honour of their Scottish equivalents, while probably the most unexpected example of global Scottish influence is the city of Blantyre in Malawi, named after the Lanarkshire birthplace of 19th-century explorer David Livingstone.

A 87

Caol Loch Aillse
Kyle of Lochalsh 1¼

Am Ploc
Plockton 6

Baile Mac Ara
Balmacara 4

(A 82)

An Gearasdan
Fort William 76

(A 887)

Inbhir Nis
Inverness 82

Macbeth

The nation of Scotland as we know it today was established in 1034 when Duncan I became king of both Alba and Strathclyde. Duncan ruled as king of Scotland until 1040, but became better known as the Duncan who was murdered in William Shakespeare's *Macbeth* – or, as it is often known, 'The Scottish Play' – written three years after the Scottish James VI's accession as king of England and Ireland in 1603. The titular antihero of the play was a warlord from Moray by the name of Mac Bethad mac Findlaich, who, after defeating Duncan, ruled Scotland from 1040 to 1057, when he was in turn defeated and killed by Duncan's son, the future Malcolm III. There are many historical inaccuracies to be found in the play: Duncan was not an elderly man when he was killed, Macbeth was not defeated at Birnam Wood in Perthshire, and, by the standards of the time, Macbeth's reign was relatively peaceful. However, thanks to Shakespeare's genius the reputations of Scotland's second king and his queen (whose real name was Gruoch) were forever tarnished, albeit with the consolation that Macbeth became the most famous Scottish monarch there has ever been.

St Margaret

Malcolm III, or Malcolm Canmore (meaning 'great chief'), became king of Scotland in 1058, one year after the death of Macbeth. He ruled a nation that now included both Lothian and Strathclyde, established Dunfermline in Fife as his new capital, and attempted to gain further land in the north of England. In 1069, Malcolm married Margaret, an exiled English Saxon princess who was born in Hungary, and together they ruled Scotland until 1093.

Margaret was a deeply devout woman and under her influence the English language would be introduced into the Scottish royal court, and the Scottish church was reformed and fully incorporated into the established Catholic Church. Three of Malcolm and Margaret's sons (Edgar, Alexander, and David) succeeded Malcolm as king, and the Canmore dynasty ruled Scotland until 1290. Queen Margaret was canonized as St Margaret in 1250 and Margaret remained one of the most popular female names in Scotland until the late 20th century, which coincidentally was exactly the same time as a certain British Prime Minister with the same name came to power.

Edinburgh

It was long thought that Scotland's capital was named after Edwin, a Northumbrian king who ruled in the 7th century. However, people have been living on the volcanic rock that today is the site of Edinburgh Castle from at least the 1st century, and the name 'Edinburgh' is now believed to derive from the ancient and straightforward Cumbric meaning of 'fort on the rock'. This fort was captured by the kings of Alba in the 10th century, and became a Scottish royal residence of Malcolm III and Margaret in the 11th century. The Edinburgh Castle that we know today dates back to the 12th century, with the chapel dedicated to Margaret being its oldest surviving building. The Old Town of Edinburgh began to be built around the Castle and was awarded royal burgh status in the 12th century, but it would not be until the 15th century that Edinburgh, then the largest town in Scotland, finally became recognized as the nation's capital.

Glasgow

Although it has never been the nation's capital, Glasgow has been the largest city in Scotland since the 19th century. According to legend, Glasgow was founded on the banks of the River Clyde in the 6th century AD by the Christian missionary and patron saint of Glasgow, St Kentigern, who was also known by the name of St Mungo (meaning 'dear friend'). The church that he built there became the site of Glasgow Cathedral, which was mostly constructed in the 13th century. When Kentigern was alive, the ancient Celtic language of Cumbric was the principal language of Strathclyde and the southwest of Scotland, and the name 'Glasgow' derives from the Cumbric, meaning 'green hollow'. St Kentigern (or St Mungo) was an important figure in the conversion of Scotland to Christianity and is said to have performed four miracles involving a bird, a tree, a bell, and a fish. These objects remain the four symbols of the city of Glasgow to this day.

Abernethy

In the 10th century the country that we now know as England was unified and began to extend its influence throughout the entire island of Britain. In 921, Constantine II became the first king of Alba to acknowledge his English counterpart, Edward the Elder, as an overlord rather than an equal, and his successors Malcolm I and Kenneth II also paid homage, but as a reward were ceded the region of Lothian in 973. By 1066 the kingdom of Alba had become the kingdom of Scotland, and when the Normans from France conquered England, the Scottish king Malcolm III saw an opportunity to extend his kingdom southwards. Malcolm invaded in 1070, but was forced back by William the Conqueror, who in turn marched into Scotland and at Abernethy in Perthshire in 1072 forced Malcolm to accept English primacy. Undeterred, the warrior Malcolm twice more waged war with England, in 1079 and 1090, but to no conclusive effect, and it was his submission at Abernethy that had the most enduring legacy on future relations between the two rival nations.

The English influence

David I, the youngest son of Malcolm and Margaret, was king of Scotland from 1124 to 1153. David had spent much of his life in England, and introduced the English feudal system of government – Norman knights and lords from England and France were awarded land and power in Scotland in return for their loyalty to the crown. David also followed the English practice of founding royal burghs, the first towns of any size in Scotland's history. However, despite this English influence, Scotland and England continued to come into conflict over who should rule northern England. This dispute culminated in 1174 in the capture and imprisonment of David's grandson, William I, who was forced to accept English primacy over all of Scotland. William and Scotland were released from this subjugation in 1189, on receipt of a large cash settlement, and the 13th century saw a gradual improvement in Anglo-Scottish relations. The Treaty of York in 1237 established the border between the two countries, which, despite many more centuries of wars, battles, and general lawlessness, has somehow remained intact to this day.

The Lion Rampant

William I ruled Scotland from 1165 until 1214. Although his reign did not feature any notable military victories, after his death William was given the nickname of 'William the Lion'. The reasons for William having such a noble epithet are uncertain, but in an era of knightly valour and heraldry are thought to be linked to his personal royal standard of a red lion standing on its hind legs against a yellow background, which is today better known as the 'Lion Rampant'.

The national flag of Scotland is the Saltire of Saint Andrew, which since 1603 has also been incorporated into the flag of the United Kingdom. However, the Lion Rampant was retained as the royal standard of the Scottish monarch, and over the centuries became so widely recognized as a national symbol that it is often seen as an alternative to the Saltire, even though officially the Lion Rampant is not a national flag and should only be flown when pertaining directly to the Crown – a distinction that today most Scots, whether royalists or not, seem determined to ignore.

Alexander III

One of the great 'what ifs?' of Scottish history took place near the Fife town of Kinghorn in 1286. Alexander III, king since 1249, was a strong and astute ruler, and his reign was the golden age of medieval Scotland. He gained the Hebrides from Norway in 1266 and cemented a new relationship of friendship with the marriage of his daughter to the Norwegian king, while his own marriage to the sister of the English king, Edward I, brought about a rare period of prosperity and peace between the two nations. However, by 1286 Alexander's only surviving heir was an infant granddaughter, Margaret, residing in Norway. With the succession in jeopardy Alexander had remarried, and with the priority of producing an heir no doubt foremost in his mind, he rode from Edinburgh to Kinghorn one stormy night to meet his wife, but in circumstances never fully explained Alexander fell from his horse and died on the rocks below. In this one moment on the cliffs of Fife, the dynasty that had ruled Scotland since its creation in 1034 came to an abrupt and sudden end, and the destiny of the nation was thrown into uncertainty for years.

ALEXANDER III.

The thistle

According to Scottish folklore, it was during the reign of Alexander III and the conflict with Norway over control of the Hebrides (which culminated in the Battle of Largs in Ayrshire in 1263) that the thistle became a national symbol of Scotland. History does not record whether it was at Largs or elsewhere, but a surprise Norwegian night attack on the unsuspecting Scots was foiled when the Norsemen were unable to make their way through a field of thistles without making numerous cries of anguish, so alerting the Scots of the impending danger. Whether this story is apocryphal or not, the thistle first appeared on Scottish coins in 1470 and has been the emblem of the *Encyclopaedia Britannica* since it was first published in Edinburgh in 1768, while the Order of the Thistle, founded in 1687, is the most senior order of chivalry in Scotland today. These are just a few examples of how the prickly and resilient Scottish plant has remained the national emblem, while the country's people have often been described in similar terms.

John Balliol

With the death of Alexander III in 1286, the crown
of Scotland passed to his granddaughter, Margaret,
'the Maid of Norway'. Although she was only three
years old, it was agreed that Margaret would be
promised in marriage to the son of Edward I of
England, so uniting the two crowns. However,
in 1290, en route from her home in Norway to
Scotland, Margaret died, and Scotland was plunged
into constitutional chaos. There were no fewer
than 13 different claimants to the crown, and with
no consensus amongst the Scottish nobility it was
decided that Edward I of England should make the
final choice. With the death of Margaret thwarting
his plans of a united kingdom, Edward agreed to the
Scots' request, but on condition that Scotland and
its new king once more accepted England's long-
standing claim of overlordship. Having received such
undertakings, in 1292 Edward selected John Balliol
as king of Scotland. However, when Balliol rebelled
in 1295 Edward deposed Scotland's only King John,
and by 1296 Edward and his army were in full military
and political control, with Scotland's history as an
independent nation seemingly at an end.

John Baliol

William Wallace

In 1297 Scotland was under the rule of Edward I of England. The Scottish king, John Balliol, had been deposed, the Stone of Destiny had been taken to London, and the Scottish nobility had sworn allegiance to their English master. Then suddenly from the west there came an obscure and lowly knight who would lead the resistance to English occupation. William Wallace defeated an English army at the Battle of Stirling Bridge in 1297, but in 1298 was defeated at the Battle of Falkirk. For seven years Wallace would remain in hiding, until in 1305 he was betrayed, captured by the English, and taken to London, where a vengeful Edward gruesomely executed him. William Wallace was only at the forefront of Scottish history for a short period of time, but his military exploits, and the cruel manner of his death, made him both a national hero and Scotland's greatest martyr. The legend of Wallace was honoured with the building of the 19th-century Wallace Monument in Stirling, and the 1995 Academy-Award-winning film *Braveheart* – although in history it was not Wallace who would be called 'Braveheart', but the next Scottish hero to fight against English rule.

Robert the Bruce

Unlike William Wallace, Robert the Bruce from Ayrshire was descended from a Norman family and was of noble birth. In 1306 he killed his nearest rival claimant to the vacant Scottish crown, John Comyn, in Dumfries, and had himself proclaimed Robert I at Scone, the first Scottish king since the deposition of John Balliol in 1296. Scotland was still under English military rule and Edward I, 'the Hammer of the Scots', once more came north to crush this latest rebellion, but died en route in 1307. Bruce had gone into hiding, where legend states that in a remote cave off the Irish coast he was inspired by a determined spider spinning its web, and resolved to try, try, and try again to defeat the occupiers. Over the next seven years he led a successful campaign to drive the English out of Scotland. By 1314, the only remaining English stronghold was at Stirling Castle. Bruce's army laid siege to Stirling, forcing the English king, Edward II, to march northwards to reassert English rule. The two armies and the two kings finally met on the 23rd of June three miles south of Stirling, at a place called Bannockburn.

Bannockburn

The Battle of Bannockburn was fought over two days on the 23rd and 24th of June 1314. It became the most famous battle in Scottish history, for not only did it prove the decisive moment in the Wars of Scottish Independence that had been fought since 1296, but it was also one of the very few occasions when Scotland actually won. At Bannockburn, the Scots, led by Robert the Bruce, defeated the larger English army of Edward II and sent the English king southwards to think again. With this victory and the capture of Stirling, Scotland was free of English occupation, although it was not until 1328, and the twin treaties of Northampton and Edinburgh, that England finally acknowledged Scottish independence. One year later, Robert I died. He was buried in Dunfermline, but as his dying wish his heart was taken to Europe to join the Crusades before it was eventually returned to Scotland, where it was buried in Melrose Abbey, the final resting place of Scotland's true 'Braveheart'.

Stirling

Although the exact site of the battlefield is uncertain, Bannockburn today lies within the city boundaries of Stirling. Due to its strategic position at the very heart of central Scotland, Stirling has played a crucial role in the history of the country. There has been a fortress at Stirling from as early as the 11th century, and in medieval Scotland to hold Stirling was a prerequisite to securing control of the nation, playing a pivotal role in the Wars of Independence as the location of both the Battle of Stirling Bridge in 1297 and Bannockburn in 1314. The present-day Stirling Castle was mostly built in the 16th century as a royal residence for the Stewarts, with the iconic Wallace Monument completed in 1869. Stirling is today, with Edinburgh, Glasgow, Aberdeen, Dundee, Inverness, and Perth, one of the seven cities of Scotland, official recognition for its enduring and symbolic importance to the history of the nation.

A national anthem

Scotland does not have an official national anthem. However, over the years there have been several patriotic Scottish songs that have been championed as possible contenders for such an honour. With lyrics by Robert Burns, 'Scots Wha Hae', which takes its inspiration from Bannockburn and the Wars of Independence, was long considered the national song of Scotland, but in recent years has been supplanted by 'Flower of Scotland', written by Roy Williamson in 1967, which also takes inspiration from the events of 1314. Since 1990, 'Flower of Scotland' has been adopted by both the Scottish national rugby union and football teams as their sporting anthem. However, in the absence of any official recognition, the debate continues about what the national anthem of Scotland should be, with many of the opinion that such an anthem should look forward, rather than 700 years into the past. And, in the interests of balance, it should also be pointed out that it was the Scottish poet James Thomson who in 1740 wrote the lyrics for the popular British patriotic anthem 'Rule Britannia'.

The Declaration of Arbroath

The most famous historic document in Scottish history was written in Latin in 1320 by Bernard of Linton, the abbot of Arbroath Abbey and the chancellor of Robert the Bruce. On the 6th of April this letter was signed by the leading nobles of Scotland and sent to Pope John XXII in an attempt to gain papal recognition for an independent Scotland with Robert as king, a recognition that had previously been denied due to the objections of the English. This letter was given the name of 'the Declaration of Arbroath' and, although a positive response was finally received in 1328, the Declaration, with its passionate espousal of Scottish independence and the right of the Scottish people to choose their own monarch, has had an enduring legacy that continues to this day. The Declaration has been credited with inspiring the American Declaration of Independence in 1776, while the 6th of April is commemorated around the world as Tartan Day, which amongst the bagpipes and kilts retains the original sentiments of the Declaration of Arbroath by honouring the independent spirit of the people of Scotland, wherever they may be.

Universities

From the 10th century to the Reformation of 1560, the Fife town of St Andrews was the religious centre of Scotland. In 1312, the immense St Andrews Cathedral (now ruined), the largest building ever constructed in medieval Scotland, was consecrated and the Bishop of St Andrews was the most important religious figure in the country. In 1410, St Andrews became the location for the founding of Scotland's first university, with students being taught theology, law, classics, and philosophy. St Andrews University was followed by Glasgow University in 1451, Aberdeen University in 1495, and the youngest of Scotland's ancient universities – and the first to be founded outside the auspices of the church – the University of Edinburgh in 1582. By the 16th century Scotland had twice the number of universities as England and a reputation for academic rigour – a reputation that had survived the retrospective discrediting of its most famous medieval scholar, the 13th-century John Duns Scotus, whose followers were derided with the name of 'dunce', which fortunately only besmirched his Borders birthplace of Duns rather than the entire country.

The Stewarts

Robert the Bruce had dedicated his reign to securing Scottish independence, but within four years of his death in 1329 the south of Scotland was once more under English occupation. Bruce's only male heir, David II, was still an infant, and his reign was to prove a troubled period in Scottish history, marked by civil war against Edward Balliol, son of John; the Black Death; and military setbacks against the English that culminated in David's capture and eleven-year imprisonment. Indeed, only England's ongoing preoccupation with France prevented Scotland's hard-fought independence from being lost. David II died in 1371 leaving no heirs, and the Scottish crown passed from the Bruce family to the Stewarts of Renfrewshire. Originally a Norman family, the Stewarts took their name from their hereditary position of High Steward of Scotland. As the son of Robert the Bruce's daughter, Marjory, Robert II became the first Stewart king in 1371, so beginning a royal dynasty that ruled Scotland for the next 300 years.

James I

In 1406, history would repeat itself when the third Stewart king, James I, became the latest Scottish monarch, after William the Lion and David II, to be captured and imprisoned by the English. Released in 1424, James was determined to make up for lost time and assert his authority on a divided, lawless nation. However, in 1437, James I was brutally assassinated in Perth, so setting the template for a century of murderous deeds and untimely and unlikely Stewart demises. In 1460, James I's son, James II, died laying siege to Roxburgh Castle: when standing too close to a cannon that accidentally exploded, he became the first monarch in the world to be killed by a firearm. And in 1488, according to the chroniclers of the time, an unknown man disguised as a priest mysteriously murdered James II's son, James III. This catalogue of misfortune was not enough to prevent yet another James, James IV, from succeeding to the throne in his father's place.

The Borders

Belying its tranquil reputation today, between the 14th and the 16th centuries, the Borders were the unquestioned 'badlands' of Scotland. A violent and highly militarized region, the location of numerous English incursions, murderous feuds between the two most powerful Borders families, the Stewarts and the Douglases, and a long history of cross-border warfare and raiding, the lawless Borders were almost impossible to govern. By the 16th century, Scotland had removed the last English garrisons from the Borders, but at the cost of Berwick-upon-Tweed, once the most prosperous and largest town in Scotland, permanently falling into English hands in 1482.

The 16th century was the heyday of the Border Reivers (a word meaning 'raiders'), who crossed the border with impunity to steal English cattle. The rule of law was finally imposed, although the legacy of four centuries of conflict in this region can still be seen in the four magnificent abbeys of Dryburgh, Jedburgh, Kelso, and Melrose, all constructed in the 12th century, and all ruins today.

The Lords of the Isles

In 1266, the islands of the Hebrides were ceded by Norway to Scotland. However, this did not mean that the Hebrides were any more under Scottish control than they had been under the rule of the Norwegians. Instead, from the 12th to the 15th centuries, the Hebrides and Scotland's mainland west coast composed a semi-autonomous region governed by the Lords of the Isles, a succession of powerful chieftains of shared Norse and Celtic heritage headed by the mighty Clan MacDonald from their stronghold on the island of Islay. The MacDonalds were the descendants of the 12th-century warlord, Somerled, and in 1336 John MacDonald of Islay became the first to gain the title of the Lord of the Isles. The Lords remained in charge of their Gaelic-speaking heartland until 1493, when James IV finally broke their power and brought the Isles under the rule of the Scottish crown. The title of the Lord of the Isles was thereafter transferred to Scotland, and continues to this day as the official Scottish name for the heir to the British throne.

James IV

James IV was king of Scotland from 1488 to 1513 and is known in history as Scotland's Renaissance Prince. James brought the Hebrides under Scottish control, built the Palace of Holyroodhouse in Edinburgh, and was a noted patron of the arts and education. James was also, according to his treasury records, the first person in history both to buy a consignment of malt whisky (in 1494) and to purchase golf clubs (in 1502). In 1503 his marriage to Margaret Tudor, the daughter of Henry VII of England, reflected the gradual improvement in Anglo-Scottish relations, but in 1513 James went to war against England and his brother-in-law, Henry VIII. On the 9th September 1513, at the Battle of Flodden in the north of England, James IV and most of the Scottish nobility were killed in one of the bloodiest defeats in Scottish history. With James IV's untimely death his one-year old son became king. Ignoring the misfortune that had befallen his predecessors, he became the fifth successive Scottish monarch to be named James.

The Auld Alliance

James IV had invaded England in 1513 in support of France, as part of a political understanding between the two countries that became known as the 'Auld Alliance', with 'auld' being the Scots word for 'old'. The French influence in Scotland had begun in the 12th century when, under the reign of David I, land and titles were given to French nobles, who became amongst the most powerful and historic families in Scotland. The political Auld Alliance began in 1295, in the reign of John Balliol, as Scotland attempted to break free from the power of Edward I and looked to France to find common cause against the English. The Alliance remained Scotland's principal foreign policy for the next 250 years, and even after the disaster of Flodden in 1513, the reign of James V saw a strengthening of the Alliance. In 1538, James V married Mary of Guise, from the most powerful family in France, and in 1542 a daughter was born, also called Mary. However, relations with England deteriorated in parallel, and in 1542 James V was defeated by an English army and died soon after, leaving his one-week-old daughter, Mary, as the new Scottish monarch.

Mary

The infant Queen Mary was the only child of James V and Mary of Guise. Furthermore, through the 1503 marriage of 'the Thistle and the Rose' between James IV and Margaret Tudor, she was the grand-niece of Henry VIII. Mary was the second female monarch of Scotland, after Margaret 'the Maid' in 1286, and, as was the case with Margaret, she immediately became a political pawn. Henry VIII proposed marriage on behalf of his son, Edward, in order to unite the crowns and the two nations. At first Scotland agreed, but then under the influence of Mary of Guise it changed its mind, infuriating a spurned Henry who launched a prolonged military campaign against the Scots that became known as 'the Rough Wooing'. Henry died in 1547, and in 1548 the young Mary was sent to France, where she was promised in marriage to François, the heir to the French throne. This was the culmination of the Auld Alliance as Scotland and France were finally united, but by the time Mary returned to Scotland in 1561 the Alliance was over, its only lasting legacy the adoption of the French spelling of 'Stuart', rather than the traditional Scottish 'Stewart'.

The Reformation

Until the 11th century, Scotland was a Celtic Christian country, but under the influence of Queen Margaret it became firmly part of the Church of Rome, with St Andrews the principal centre of Scottish Catholicism. However, by the early 16th century the movement for religious reform was gathering pace. In 1528, Patrick Hamilton became Scotland's first Protestant martyr, and by the 1550s, Protestantism, with its demands for church services to be conducted in Scots rather than Latin and for the church to be less corrupt and more godly, had become popular throughout the Scottish Lowlands. With the support of dissenting nobles (who were opposed to the rule of Mary of Guise as regent and the French troops based in Scotland), a Protestant army marched on Edinburgh in 1560 and forced the French to surrender. A Reformation Parliament was called and the Catholic Church was abolished, to be replaced by a new, national Protestant church that was called the Church of Scotland or, as it is known in Scotland, 'the Kirk'.

Queen of Scots

In 1559, the teenage Mary, Queen of Scots also became Queen of France, when her even younger husband was crowned François II. If François had lived, the history of Scotland – and the life of Mary – would have been very different, but the sickly François died within a year, so ending all hopes of a grand Franco-Scottish empire. In 1561, the widowed Mary returned to Scotland, a devout Catholic in a country that had turned radically Protestant in her absence. Mary was Queen of Scots for six tumultuous years, in which time she was disastrously married twice – to Henry Stewart, Lord Darnley, and to Patrick Hepburn, Earl of Bothwell – and gave birth in 1566 to her only child, James. It was the murder of Darnley, the father of James, in 1567 that was her final undoing, with Bothwell and Mary herself being the principal suspects. It was never proved that Mary was involved in the murder of her second husband or if she was a willing partner in the marriage to her third, but the scandal was too much for the Scottish nobility. Mary was forced to abdicate in favour of her one-year-old son, and at the age of 26 the reign of Scotland's most dramatic, and ultimately doomed, monarch was over.

The Royal Mile

To the bemusement of many, the historic Edinburgh street that runs from Edinburgh Castle to the Palace of Holyroodhouse and the new Scottish Parliament is not officially called the Royal Mile, but is instead a series of connecting streets: Castlehill, Lawnmarket, High Street, and Canongate, 1.1 miles long (or an obsolete old Scottish mile). The Palace of Holyroodhouse, built in the 16th century by the Stewart kings, is today the official Scottish residence of the British monarch, and takes its name from the ruined 12th-century Holyrood Abbey (with 'rood' being the Scots word for 'cross'). On the High Street stands the 14th-century St Giles' Cathedral (named after St Giles, the patron saint of Edinburgh), which in the 16th century was at the centre of the Scottish Reformation. In 1560, the radical preacher John Knox became the first Protestant minister of St Giles' or, as it was known, the High Kirk of Scotland. The High Kirk remains the official name of St Giles' Cathedral, as the term 'cathedral' was only briefly used in the 17th century. However, as with the unofficial 'Royal Mile', the technically ambiguous 'St Giles' Cathedral' has now become the accepted norm.

Presbyterianism

The Church of Scotland, or Kirk, established in 1560, was Protestant, but noticeably different in tenor and structure from its Protestant English contemporary, the Church of England. Scottish Protestants, such as John Knox, were followers of John Calvin, and were advocates of the Calvinist principles of worship, hard work, and independence from the crown. Priests and bishops were abolished as all remnants of Catholicism were swept away, replaced by a pyramid structure where 'elders', or 'presbyters', ran their own church and chose their own minister. Individual churches would send representatives to a regional 'presbytery', and an annual General Assembly in Edinburgh decided on national church policy. However, the monarch was not the head of the Church of Scotland – in contrast to its English counterpart – since Presbyterians are only answerable to God.

This independence from the crown was challenged by successive monarchs as Scotland was embroiled in 130 years of religious conflict between King and Kirk. Finally, in 1690, Presbyterianism was recognized as the only national form of Protestantism in Scotland.

The Union of the Crowns

In 1568, Mary, the former Queen of Scots, fled to England and sought sanctuary from the English queen, Elizabeth, who was also her first cousin (once removed). Elizabeth was unmarried, Protestant, and the last of the Tudor dynasty, which meant that Mary, her unwanted Catholic guest, was also next in line to the English throne. For 19 years, Elizabeth, who refused to meet her cousin, held Mary captive in England. However, for as long as Mary lived she remained a threat to Elizabeth's rule, and eventually, in 1587, Mary was executed on Elizabeth's orders.

Mary's son, James VI, king of Scotland since 1567, had not seen his mother since he was one year old. Brought up a Protestant, James did not allow Mary's death to stand in the way of his ambitions to become king of England, as he was now heir to the crown. He waited patiently until Elizabeth's death, whereupon in 1603 he left for London, where he was crowned James I of England and Ireland. Thus, after nearly 700 years of claims of English primacy, it was a Scottish king, and the son of a queen who nobody wanted, who united the crowns of England and Scotland.

James VI & I

On the 24th of March 1603, the crowns of England
and Scotland were united under James VI of Scotland,
who gave himself the title of James I of Great Britain
and Ireland. A new union flag, incorporating both
the Scottish Saltire and the English flag of St George
was introduced, and in 1607 James attempted to
strengthen this union by bringing the parliaments of
Scotland and England together, but was rebuffed by
an English parliament that was reluctant to share its
trading wealth with its Scottish neighbours. The reign
of James was notable for the establishment of the
first English colony in America (named 'Jamestown'
after the king), the Protestant settlement of Northern
Ireland, the Gunpowder Plot of 1605, and the
publication in 1611 of the Authorized Version of the
Bible in English (or, as it is better known, the King
James Bible). In England, the rule of James I from
1603 to 1625 became the glorious Jacobean Age, but in
Scotland James VI was an absent king, returning only
once to his homeland. A complex and contradictory
figure, James earned the double-edged epithet of
'the wisest fool in Christendom', an unfortunate
legacy for the man who changed British history.

The Covenanters

The last king of Scotland to be born in Scotland was Charles I, who succeeded his father, James VI, in 1625. Born in Dunfermline in 1600, Charles followed his father's belief in the divine right of kings to rule, but lacked James' political pragmatism. As kings of England, James and Charles were also heads of the Church of England, but their attempts to reform the Church of Scotland along the lines of the English model were opposed by Scottish Presbyterians, who maintained their core belief that no monarch should be head of the Kirk. In 1637, Charles imposed an English Common Prayer Book and reimposed bishops on the recalcitrant Scots. In response, a National Covenant was drawn up in Greyfriars Churchyard in Edinburgh in 1638, protesting against Charles' interference in Scottish religious affairs. Supporters of the Covenant were known as 'Covenanters', and in 1639 and 1640 Covenanter armies marched into England in 'the Bishops' Wars', forcing Charles to reverse his policies. The Covenanters had succeeded in their goal, but with the unexpected consequence that they had so weakened their king that within two years all of Britain was engulfed in civil war.

COVENANT REST
PSALMS
CXXXII 14

Civil Wars

Erroneously known as the 'English Civil Wars', the conflicts from 1642 to 1651 between supporters and opponents of Charles I were a series of power struggles in which Scotland played a prominent yet contradictory role. In 1643, the Scottish Parliament, dominated by Covenanters, allied itself with the forces of the English Parliament and the two jointly signed the Solemn League and Covenant, which promised the introduction of Presbyterianism in England in return for Scottish military support against the king. A Scottish army invaded England in 1644, tipping the balance in favour of the Parliamentary forces. In 1646, Charles surrendered to the Scots, who eventually handed the king over to his English opponents. However, in 1648 an increasingly divided Scotland changed sides and sent another army into England, but this time to fight on Charles' behalf. The Scots were defeated at Preston in 1648, and the following year their Scottish-born king, whom they had fought both against and then belatedly for, was executed. He was the second Stewart monarch to suffer such a fate, 62 years after his grandmother, Mary, Queen of Scots.

Parliament

Despite the Union of the Crowns and the departure of James VI in 1603, Scotland remained a separate, independent nation with a separate, independent parliament. The first record of a Scottish Parliament was in 1235, and by the 14th century the meeting of a parliament, summoned by the monarch of the day, had become an established, if irregular, event in the governance of the country. In medieval Scotland members of parliament came from the 'Three Estates' that made up the highest echelons of society (bishops from the church, lords and nobles who owned the land, and representatives from the growing towns and burghs). Parliament had the power to decide on taxation, legislation, and foreign policy, but with no official Scottish capital, parliaments were held in St Andrews, Edinburgh, Perth, Stirling, or wherever the king decreed. It was not until 1639 that the Scottish Parliament found a permanent home, at Parliament House, next to St Giles' Cathedral in Edinburgh. This act also conferred on Edinburgh the honour of becoming Scotland's capital city.

The Stuarts

In England, the Stewarts had adopted the name of Stuart after the Union of the Crowns in 1603. After Charles I's execution in 1649, England became a commonwealth republic ruled by the English parliament. The Scottish Parliament, realizing that England was never going to adopt Presbyterianism, supported the Stuart cause, whose figurehead Charles I's son, also named Charles, landed in Scotland in 1650. In response, the English, led by Oliver Cromwell, invaded Scotland and defeated a larger Scottish army at Dunbar in East Lothian in 1650. Charles II was proclaimed king at Scone in 1651 – the last monarch to be crowned in Scotland – but by the end of 1651, he had fled the country and the Civil Wars were over. By 1653, Cromwell had succeeded where all his royal predecessors had failed and fully incorporated Scotland into a new British Commonwealth, with the Scottish Parliament abolished, the Church of Scotland diminished, and all power residing in London. However, only seven years later, in 1660, the Commonwealth was over, and the Stuarts were restored under Charles II, with Scotland and England once more separate kingdoms.

The Kirk

Charles II was king of Scotland from 1660 to 1685, but never returned to his northern kingdom. The Scottish Parliament in Edinburgh was restored, but the Covenanters and Presbyterians had lost power. Charles reintroduced bishops and English Protestantism in the form of the Episcopalian Church, so intensifying religious conflict that this became known as 'the Killing Time' on account of the escalating persecution and violence. In 1685, Charles II died and was succeeded by his Catholic brother James VII (or James II). However, in 1688, the English Parliament overthrew James and invited his Protestant daughter, Mary, and her Dutch Protestant husband, William of Orange, to jointly assume the throne in his place. The Scottish Parliament played no part in the English revolution, but in 1689 offered the Scottish crown to William and Mary, on the condition that the Church of Scotland was to be independent of the crown and exclusively Presbyterian. William, after whom the Highland town of Fort William is named, accepted, but with the proviso that other Protestant faiths were to be tolerated, and after 130 years of division, a lasting religious settlement came to Scotland, but with the new reality that state and church were now independent of each other.

Jacobites

The term 'Jacobites' refers to *Jacobus*, the Latin form of 'James'. Between 1394 and 1625 there were six Scottish Stewart monarchs who shared that name, but the Jacobite cause does not equate to either the House of Stewart, or Scotland itself. Instead, Jacobites were specifically supporters of the deposed James VII and his son, James 'the Old Pretender', both of whom were Catholics and neither born in a Scotland that was now overwhelmingly Protestant. Furthermore, it was James VII's own Stuart daughters – first Mary in 1689, and from 1702, Queen Anne – who had displaced him as monarch. Therefore, the Jacobite cause of restoring James VII and his son to the thrones of England, Scotland, and Ireland was never restricted to any one nation, one religious faith, or even one royal family. However, despite the Stuarts leaving Scotland and their Stewart name behind in 1603, it was in Scotland, where they had ruled for 300 years, that the Jacobites gained their greatest support and exacerbated a division in Scotland that had existed from even before the first Stewart king.

The Highlands

Until the 18th century Scotland was a country that was divided geographically, politically, culturally, and linguistically in two. The Lowlands were where the monarch (until 1603) and Parliament resided, towns and trade flourished, and Scots and English were the spoken and written languages. The Highlands and Islands, however, remained almost entirely rural, with no equivalent large towns. Gaelic was still the overwhelming language, and power resided with the dominant landowning families (or clans), who administered local justice through ancient rights called 'heritable jurisdictions'. The Highlands and Islands had overwhelmingly converted to Protestantism after the Reformation of 1560, but Catholicism had survived there too, and the Episcopalian form of Protestantism, as introduced by the Stuart kings, remained popular even after the Church of Scotland became Presbyterian in 1690. Politically, the Highlands and Islands had been incorporated into the Scottish crown with the fall of the Lords of the Isles in 1493, but they remained a distinct and very different land, far removed from the events of London and Edinburgh.

Clans

Scottish surnames take many forms. The four most popular Scottish surnames (Smith, Brown, Thomson, and Wilson) are Lowland names, deriving from Scots or English, and representing an occupation (Smith), a description (Brown), and two patronymic forms (son of Thomas; son of William). Lowland surnames originated with the Norman nobles of the 12th century, but in the Highlands and Islands surnames are associated with the historic 'clan' system, with the Gaelic word 'clann' meaning 'children'. Clans dominated Highland and Island society until the 18th century, with their chieftains owning land, administering justice and leading their clans into battle. Clan surnames were derived from Gaelic and were commonly also patronymic forms, with the prefix 'mac' meaning 'son of'. The two most powerful Highland clans were the MacDonalds and the Campbells from Argyll, whose rivalry reached an infamous nadir in 1692 with the Massacre of Glencoe in Lochaber. Campbell soldiers, acting on government orders, killed 38 MacDonalds in their homes after first accepting MacDonald hospitality, a grievous Highland insult that is remembered to this day.

Darien

From time immemorial Scots have been leaving their homeland in search of a better life. By the 17th century there were estimated to be 30,000 Scots living in Poland, while in Ireland Scottish settlers had created a Protestant majority in the north of the island. At the same time, England was establishing a colonial and trading empire in the Americas and Asia. In 1695, the Scottish Parliament decided to launch its own trading company. The first Scottish colony was the Darien peninsula of Panama, and in 1698 financier William Paterson, having raised substantial levels of investment, set sail for Central America. The Darien Scheme was an unmitigated disaster for Scotland. The first colonists were decimated by disease, the English obstructed the Scots in their attempts to trade, and in 1700 Darien was abandoned. The failure of the Darien Scheme left Scottish hopes of an independent empire in ruins and brought the Scottish economy close to bankruptcy – a national humiliation that perversely brought new opportunities for those Scots who sought a very different form of constitutional change.

The line of succession

The failure of the Darien Scheme in 1700 was a considerable setback for a Scottish Parliament that had been emboldened to look optimistically to the future after the 1690 religious settlement confirming Presbyterianism as the national faith, the defeat of the first Jacobite rebellion of 1689–90, and the accession of William and Mary, absentee monarchs with little interest in Scotland. After Darien, a weakened Scotland found itself once more under threat from England, with the royal line of succession becoming a pressing concern. Queen Anne, a daughter of James VII, had ascended the throne in 1702, but with no surviving heirs she was the last of the Protestant Stuarts. With the restoration of the Catholic Stuart line deemed unthinkable, the English Parliament had identified the Protestant Hanoverian family from Germany, descended from Elizabeth, the daughter of James VI, as the next in line. However, for this line of succession to be peacefully achieved the English required the acquiescence of the Scots. Such an agreement might previously have seen the threat of military force, but in 1702 that threat was replaced by a more potent means of persuasion: hard cash.

The Act of Union

Negotiations for a union of the English and Scottish Parliaments lasted from 1702 until 1706. Initially the Scottish Parliament was opposed to union, and the Scottish public, as far as we know, was consistently hostile, but had no say. However, as the English imposed ever more restrictive trading sanctions on the already impoverished Scottish economy, and members of the Scottish Parliament were offered financial inducements to support union, a formal treaty was agreed in 1706 and presented to the Scottish Parliament for ratification. On the 16th of January 1707, by a vote of 110 to 68, the Scottish Parliament agreed to its own dissolution. Scotland's systems of local government, law, education, and religion were all retained by the Act of Union, but all other powers were transferred to the English, now United Kingdom, Parliament in London. There were riots on the streets of Scotland's major towns, but no uprising. On the 1st of May 1707, the unconsulted Scottish population awoke to find themselves British citizens, as nearly 700 years of Scottish independence came to an anticlimactic end.

Language

The long, inexorable decline of Gaelic, the language of the Gaels, dates back to the 11th century when the kingdom of Alba became the kingdom of Scotland, and English, French, Latin, and Scots became the languages of the crown, the church, and the nobility. By the 15th century, Scots, which was derived from Old English and was the historic language of Lothian and the Borders, had replaced Gaelic in the southwest, permanently isolating and differentiating Scottish Gaelic from its Irish equivalent. However, this victory for Lowland Scots proved relatively short-lived, as with the union of the crowns and of the parliaments English superseded Scots as the language of Scotland in the new Great Britain. Scots, or 'Lallans', remained the language (or dialect) of Lowland Scotland, with regional variations, such as 'Doric' in the northeast, but English became the official language of education, law, and the state. Gaelic, still spoken by half the Scottish population, was restricted to the 'Gaidhealtachd', the land of the Gaels in the Highlands and Islands, politically and culturally removed from the rest of the country, and fatally susceptible to the battle cries of the past.

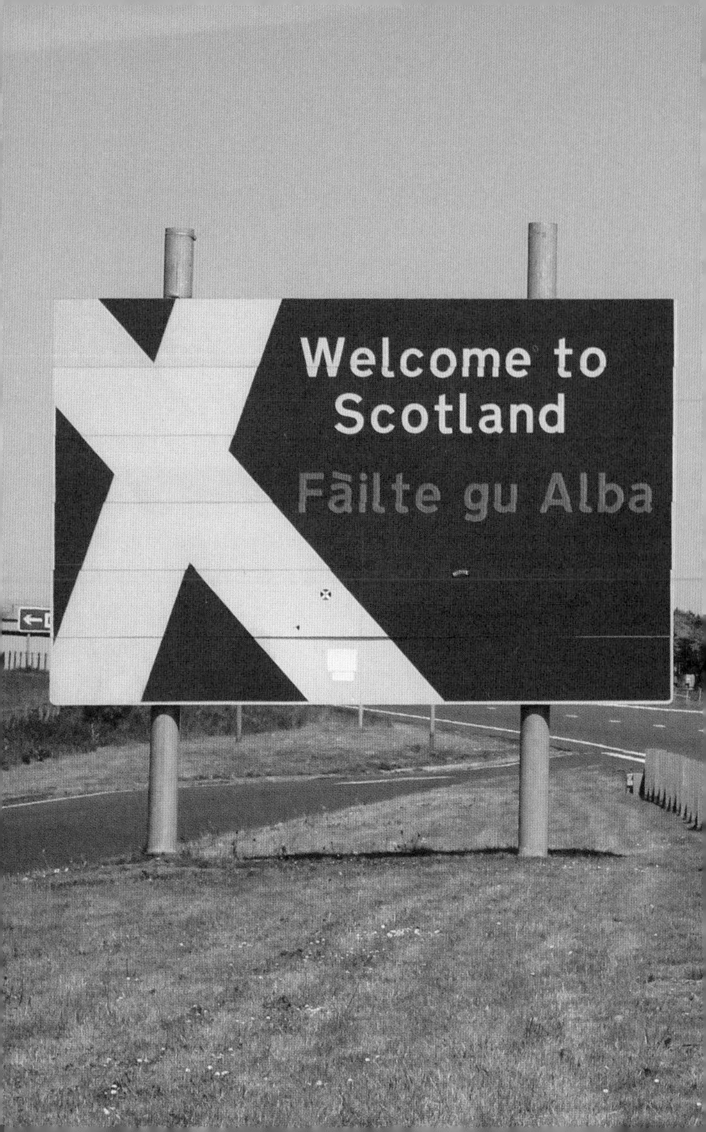
Welcome to
Scotland
Fàilte gu Alba

Rebellion

There were four Jacobite rebellions after the Act of Union of 1707, each attempting to place James 'the Old Pretender' on the British throne. In 1708, perhaps the best opportunity was lost when a French-backed invasion was averted by bad weather off the Scottish coast. In September 1715, a year after the death of Queen Anne and the accession of the Hanoverian George I, the Jacobite standard was raised in Aberdeenshire. Although they gained support in the Highlands and the northeast of Scotland, the Jacobites found minimal sympathy elsewhere. By the time James belatedly arrived at Peterhead in January 1716, the rebellion was all but over, and a month later 'the Old Pretender' returned to exile. There was another short-lived rising in 1719, swiftly repressed, and it appeared that the time for a Jacobite restoration had come and gone, if it had ever truly existed in the first place. Britain was at peace, the Highlands were pacified, the French had lost interest in the Jacobite cause, and not even James Stuart would have expected that 26 years later the Jacobite standard would once more be raised in his name.

Bonnie Prince Charlie

Charles Edward Stuart, the son of James 'the Old Pretender', was born in Rome in 1720, and arrived in Scotland without warning in August 1745. The Jacobite standard was raised at Glenfinnan in Lochaber in the name of his still-living father, but 30 years after the 1715 rebellion, there was less support from the Highland clans. Undeterred, and with few government forces standing in his way, Charles and his Highland army marched unopposed into Edinburgh in September and won a battle at nearby Prestonpans in East Lothian. However, they did not stay long, for it was not the vacant crown of Scotland that was the prize. The Jacobites marched into England but gained no additional support, and with a large government force approaching they turned back at Derby and retreated northwards. By January 1746, the remnants of Charles' Jacobite army, numbering no more than 5,000, were just outside Inverness, with nowhere else to run and a British army of 9,000 in inexorable pursuit.

Culloden

On the 16th of April 1746, the last battle, to date, on the British mainland was fought at Culloden, near Inverness. The battle of Culloden has become mythologized as the final battle between England and Scotland, but in reality there were as many, if not more, Scots fighting for the British as there were for the Jacobites, as the Lowlanders were overwhelmingly opposed to the rebellion, while the Highland clans were divided about the wisdom of supporting such a misguided campaign. The Jacobites were outnumbered by nearly two to one at Culloden, and were swiftly and ruthlessly routed. Charles survived and fled westwards, remaining on the run for four months before being rescued by a French ship near Arisaig in August. The flight of Charles, and his crossing to Skye disguised as Flora Macdonald's surprisingly tall maid, immortalized him as 'Bonnie Prince Charlie', the romantic prince across the water, and yet another flawed Stuart hero. However, the real Charles would live another, mostly dissolute, 42 years, until his death in 1788, leaving no legitimate heirs to continue a cause that the Highlands had long since come to bitterly regret.

THE BATTLE
OF CULLODEN
WAS FOUGHT ON THIS MOOR
16TH APRIL 1746.

THE GRAVES OF THE
GALLANT HIGHLANDERS
WHO FOUGHT FOR
SCOTLAND & PRINCE CHARLIE,
ARE MARKED BY THE NAMES
OF THEIR CLANS.

After Culloden

Leading the British army at Culloden was the Duke of Cumberland, son of the king, George II. Cumberland was determined to destroy the Jacobites once and for all, and in the aftermath of the battle ordered his troops to take no prisoners, a policy so brutal that despite being the victor he became forever known as 'the Butcher' Cumberland. After the 1715 rebellion, the British government had responded pragmatically to the Highland problem by tasking General George Wade to build military forts and roads, and by the creation of the Black Watch in 1725, the first Highland British regiment. However, after the 1745 rebellion, the government was determined to subjugate the Highland clans, regardless of whether they supported the Jacobites or not. Symbolically, they prohibited the kilt and the official use of Gaelic, but the abolition of heritable jurisdictions in 1748 saw the collapse of the centuries-old clan system and Highland economy. In the first national census of 1755, half of the Scottish population lived in the north of the country, but in the aftermath of Culloden many now saw emigration as their only choice.

TO THE MEMORY OF
OFFICERS
COMMISSIONED OFFICERS
OF
THE BLACK WATCH

America

In 1629, the first Scottish colony was founded in North America. Although it was soon abandoned, it bequeathed the name 'Nova Scotia', Latin for 'New Scotland', to the future Canadian province. After the Act of Union of 1707, Scotland gained access to England's growing American empire, and thousands of Scots made the journey across the Atlantic to the New World. The Scots were only a small minority of the immigrant population, but they played a disproportionately important role in the American War of Independence of 1775–83. John Paul Jones (commander of the American Navy), James Craik (physician general of the American army), John Witherspoon (president of Princeton University), and James Wilson (co-author of the American Constitution) were only four of the prominent Scots-born Americans who helped found the United States, with Witherspoon and Wilson among the signatories of the Declaration of Independence in 1776. So many Americans of Scottish origin fought on the American side that the British often described the conflict as a 'Presbyterian War', with Scots demonstrating a rebellious spirit long since dissipated in Scotland itself.

The Enlightenment

By the end of the 18th century, the great constitutional and theological battles of the previous century had been settled. Scotland was part of Great Britain, power resided in London, and the Jacobite cause was over, with the unfortunate Highlands paying a heavy price in retribution. However, Scotland retained its separate legal and education systems, and in the 18th century saw a flourishing of intellectual thought that became known as the Scottish Enlightenment. This was the European Age of Reason, an era in which scientists, writers, and philosophers attempted to understand and explain the world, and Scotland – and specifically Edinburgh – was at its unlikely epicentre. Economist Adam Smith, philosopher David Hume, geologist James Hutton, and scientist Joseph Black were but four of the enlightened Scots who discussed and re-evaluated the meaning of life in Edinburgh's Old Town. The Scottish Enlightenment established Scotland's international reputation for academic excellence and scientific rigour. Having been removed from the concerns of national politics, Scots turned instead to answering the greater calling of changing the world.

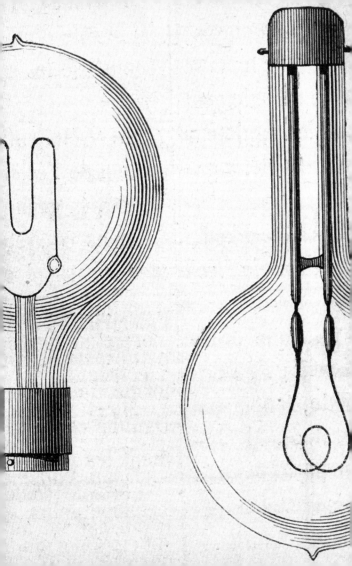

Hume and Hutton

The figure who became most synonymous with the Scottish Enlightenment was Edinburgh-born philosopher and historian David Hume. His most influential work, *A Treatise of Human Nature*, was first published in 1739, and throughout his life Hume advocated the merits of rigorous intellectual debate on all aspects of life, knowledge, and religion. This sceptical philosophical viewpoint was lauded internationally, but placed him in conflict with the Church of Scotland and the prevailing moral philosophy of the time. Equally controversial was the publication in 1788 of Edinburgh geologist James Hutton's *Theory of the Earth*, in which, after years of studying the different rock formations in Scotland, Hutton first proposed the radical and blasphemous conclusion that the Earth was significantly older than the 6,000 years stated in the Bible. Hutton, who is today honoured as 'the father of geology', would not live to see his theories accepted, but, as with the similarly criticized Hume, would have his right to say the unthinkable tolerated in the spirit of intellectual debate, so demonstrating how enlightened the Scottish Enlightenment actually was.

Adam Smith

In the 18th century the city of Glasgow had rapidly grown through the tobacco trade with America, an economic expansion that had a major influence on the thinking of a Professor of Moral Philosophy at Glasgow University. Adam Smith was born in Kirkcaldy in Fife, and in 1776 he published *Inquiry into the Nature and Causes of the Wealth of Nations*, a work that had taken him ten years to write. In *The Wealth of Nations* Smith outlined his views on trade, commerce, taxation, the workforce, political and moral responsibilities, and – his most famous phrase – 'the division of labour'. Published at the beginning of the Industrial Revolution, *The Wealth of Nations*, with its message of wealth being derived from greater and freer trade, had a global impact that continues to this day. Smith influenced both subsequent imperialism and Marxism and his work became a template for modern capitalism, with a legacy that saw him proclaimed the founder of modern economics, and an enduring reputation, both good and ill, that makes him, even more than his contemporaries Hume and Hutton, the most significant figure of the Scottish Enlightenment.

Edinburgh's New Town

In the late 18th century, Edinburgh was the centre of the Scottish Enlightenment, but the city itself had seen better days. With the dissolution of the Scottish Parliament in 1707, Edinburgh had lost its political power, and the historic Old Town of Edinburgh had become increasingly overcrowded and squalid, no matter how many extra storeys were built. In 1767, work began on the development of Edinburgh's New Town, as designed by architect James Craig, a grand residential suburb for the most affluent of the population. The polluted Nor Loch was drained and turned into today's Princes Street Gardens, while to the north of the loch work on the New Town continued until 1820. George Street, named after George III, was the original centrepiece of the New Town, but in the 19th century shops appeared on the less fashionable Princes Street, opposite the Gardens, and this now superseded George Street as Edinburgh's principal thoroughfare. In the planning stage, Princes Street had been called St Giles' Street, after Edinburgh's patron saint, but royal protocol dictated otherwise and Princes Street was named after George III's sons, Prince George and Prince Frederick.

Robert Burns

Scotland's most revered cultural figure was born on the 25th of January 1759 in Alloway, Ayrshire. His literary career from the publication of his first poems in 1786 to his death in 1796 was relatively brief, but in ten years he produced a body of work that has rarely been surpassed. Burns wrote primarily in Scots, but the tenderness, humour, patriotism, and insight into the human spirit that shone through his writing found an audience far beyond Scotland. Burns did not make his fortune from poetry, and his personal life was perennially chaotic, but through such poems as 'To a Mouse', 'A Man's a Man for a' That', and 'Tam O' Shanter', the 'ploughman poet' became, after his death, Scotland's national bard and an iconic figure for the Scottish diaspora, who celebrate his birthday on Burns' Night, the alternative national day of Scotland. The greatest example of Burns' universal appeal is 'Auld Lang Syne'. Translated as 'old long since', 'Auld Lang Syne' is today sung on Hogmanay (the 31st of December) to usher in the New Year throughout the English-speaking world, despite the fact that few, even in Scotland, fully understand the Scots words that they are singing.

Haggis

For a country often derided for its diet, Scottish cuisine has a long and noble history, albeit one predicated more on practical necessity than any culinary pretensions. From the 17th to the early 20th centuries oats were a staple food crop of Scotland, with porridge, made from oatmeal boiled in salted water, a traditional, simple, and filling dish that while not exclusive to Scotland became synonymous with the Calvinist aspect of the Scottish psyche. Oatmeal is also a principal ingredient of haggis, which through its association with Burns Night and the humorous Burns poem 'Address to a Haggis' has become recognized as Scotland's national dish. Of unknown, and perhaps English, origin, haggis consists of the chopped-up liver, heart, and lungs of a sheep, mixed with oatmeal and suet, and then cooked in a sheep's stomach. On Burns Night haggis is served with 'neeps and tatties' (turnips and potatoes), but for those who find the traditional ingredients of haggis somewhat off-putting, excellent vegetarian options are also available.

Ossian

Between 1760 and 1765, a series of epic poems was published purporting to chronicle the legendary exploits of Fingal, a heroic Celtic warrior, as told by his son Ossian, and translated by James Macpherson. The Ossian poems were the literary phenomenon of the age and a precursor to the coming era of European Romanticism. Even when it became clear that there were no ancient Gaelic manuscripts involved and that Macpherson was instead the sole author, Ossian's enduring influence on how Scotland, and particularly the Highlands, were perceived continued into the 19th century and the *Hebrides Overture*, or 'Fingal's Cave', composed by Felix Mendelssohn in 1832. In 1814 Edinburgh-born author Walter Scott reinforced this re-imagining of the Highlands with the publication of *Waverley*, a best-selling historical novel that depicted the Jacobites and Highlanders in a heroic and sympathetic light. This was followed in 1818 by *Rob Roy*, based on the real-life exploits of Highland outlaw Rob Roy MacGregor. The success of *Rob Roy* made Loch Lomond and the Trossachs an international tourist destination, but for Walter Scott an even greater legacy lay ahead.

Walter Scott

In his home town of Edinburgh, Walter Scott is commemorated today with the imposing Scott Monument that overlooks the Waverley Railway Station, named in honour of his breakthrough novel, and it was in Edinburgh in 1822 that he organized the event that made him arguably the most influential Scot of the 19th century. No reigning monarch had visited Scotland since 1641, demonstrating just how much of a constitutional backwater the country now was. There was therefore considerable excitement at the impending arrival of George IV in 1822, a mere 181 years after the last royal visit. Scott was placed in charge of 'the King's Jaunt' and turned the royal visit into a cavalcade of tartan Highland romanticism, even persuading the corpulent George to wear a kilt that was widely reported as being somewhat on the short side. At the Battle of Culloden, 76 years before, the Lowlanders had finally defeated and destroyed the Highland way of life, but thanks to the creative imagination of Walter Scott, it was a fictionalized Highlands that led to the stereotypical representation of Scotland that we know today.

Tartan

The origins of tartan date back many centuries to the patterns of different coloured stripes on woollen cloth, known as 'setts', and worn by Highlanders as a 'plaid', that was wrapped around the middle and over the shoulder, the forerunner of the modern kilt. After Culloden, the wearing of plaid was prohibited from 1746 to 1782, with the exception of the Highland regiments in the British army. George IV confirmed the rehabilitation of tartan with the wearing of a kilt in 1822, but as with the coordinator of the royal visit, Walter Scott, modern tartan was very much a Lowland invention. To achieve the colourful spectacle, Scott required the weaving firm of William Wilson from Bannockburn to create tartan designs for Scotland's historic clans and families, both Highland and Lowland, regardless of any historical precedent. It was, therefore, 1822 that saw the beginning of modern Highland dress, but as invented by Lowland Scots, with the kilt replacing plaid, accompanied by a sporran (Gaelic for 'purse') and the Highland weapons of the 'dirk' and the 'sgian dubh' (Gaelic for 'black knife') understandably only worn on ceremonial occasions.

Regiments

For centuries before 1707, Scottish soldiers fought in the Scottish Army and as mercenaries across the battlefields of Europe in the service of whoever would pay them. After the Act of Union, however, they gained employment in the British army. The oldest continuing Scottish regiment, the Royal Scots, was first raised in 1633, and along with the King's Own Scottish Borderers (first raised in 1689), recruits from the Lowlands. These two historic regiments are now amalgamated as the Royal Scots Borderers, one of five current battalions in the Royal Regiment of Scotland. The remaining four battalions (the Black Watch, the Highlanders, the Royal Highland Fusiliers, and the Argyll and Sutherlands) are all of Highland and northeastern origin, with the oldest being the Black Watch, which was first raised in 1725, only ten years after the 1715 Jacobite Rebellion. In the 19th century, Scottish regiments fought in the Napoleonic Wars, the Crimea, India, and wherever the British Empire sent them. In 1854, the famous 'Thin Red Line' that repulsed the Russians at the Battle of Balaclava was made up of the 93rd Highlanders, wearing red coats and kilts, loyal British soldiers, but still proudly Scots.

Bagpipes

Scottish regiments have historically formed a disproportionately high percentage of the British army, and since the 18th century have been allowed to maintain their distinct Scottish identity. Today, each of the five surviving regular Scottish battalions in the Royal Regiment of Scotland, whether Highland or Lowland, wears its own regimental tartan, either as kilts or trousers, known as 'trews', and each has its own regimental pipe band, consisting of bagpipes and drums. The origins of the great Highland bagpipe are unclear, but date back to at least the 15th century. Bagpipes themselves predate the 15th century, and at one time were popular throughout Europe and Asia, but through their adoption by Scottish regiments they have become especially associated with Scotland. Highland bagpipe music is known in Gaelic as 'piobaireach' ('pibroch' in English), and can be played as laments or dance music, but it is in a military context that it remains best known, with the Royal Edinburgh Military Tattoo, first held on the esplanade of Edinburgh Castle (the headquarters of the Royal Regiment of Scotland) in 1950, being its ceremonial annual showcase.

James Watt

In 1765, at Glasgow University, an instrument-maker from Greenock attempted to repair a steam pump, and realized that by adding a separate steam condenser he could vastly improve the design. With this one discovery, which he patented in 1769, James Watt not only invented the modern steam engine, but kick-started the period of history that we know as the Industrial Revolution. Watt moved to Birmingham in England, where he improved on his steam condenser with a double-action steam engine, and coined the term 'horsepower' to demonstrate the efficiency and power of his new invention. Over the next century, Watt's engine transformed industry first in Britain and then in the rest of the world, bringing unparalleled social and economic change as people left the countryside to find work in the factories and mines that were driven by his machines. The Lowlands of Scotland, with rich natural resources of coal and iron and a growing textiles industry, were at the forefront of the Industrial Revolution in the late 18th century, but Watt's legacy was felt across the world, and he is honoured today through the 'watt', the universally recognized unit of power.

A merchant city

After 1707, Scottish merchants gained access to the English trading routes to the Americas, with the city of Glasgow being geographically best placed to capitalize on these lucrative markets. In the 18th century, tobacco was the principal trade commodity, but after the American War of Independence it was replaced by equally profitable cotton and sugar. Tobacco, cotton, and sugar were all predicated on slavery, and while Glasgow was not directly involved in the slave trade, there were no moral qualms about exploiting slave labour. By the end of the 19th century, Glasgow was the richest and fastest-growing city in Scotland, with the historic merchant city expanding westwards, and the deepening of the River Clyde allowing more ships to access the city's port. In the early 19th century, with the Industrial Revolution gathering pace, Glasgow saw further growth as its economy, previously based on imports, now concentrated on industry and manufacturing and required an ever larger workforce. Edinburgh was still the nominal Scottish capital, but for the first time Glasgow was now the largest city and the commercial and industrial powerhouse for the coming age.

Textiles

In the first half of the 19th century, the textile business was the predominant industry in Scotland. In the east of Scotland there was linen, and in the Borders there was wool (with the misreading of the Scots word 'tweel', meaning 'weave', as 'tweed' beginning the fashion for waterproof woollen country wear). Overall, however, it was cotton that was king, imported from America to the numerous mills and factories in the west of Scotland. The most famous Scottish cotton mill was the village of New Lanark in Lanarkshire. Founded by David Dale in 1784, New Lanark was taken over by his Welsh son-in-law, Robert Owen, in 1800. Owen was a social reformer who believed that by providing housing, education, and improved working conditions to his employees and their families he could create a better society, as well as improving productivity. Disheartened that his altruistic policies were not adopted by other mill-owners, Owen left Scotland in 1825. However, the legacy of New Lanark became an inspiration for both the cooperative and socialist movements, and the village is now preserved as a World Heritage Site.

The Highland Clearances

There was no Industrial Revolution in the Highlands and Islands. After the collapse of the clan system, land was divided between government-approved 'lairds' (the Scots word for 'landowners'). In the Lowlands, 18th-century agricultural improvements increased the productivity of the land, but in the less fertile Highlands, where agriculture had been based on cattle, the new lairds introduced sheep farming, and their tenants were 'persuaded' to leave their homes to make way for the new arrivals. These 'Clearances' began in the 1770s and reached their peak between 1810 and 1850, with the most infamous example being the eviction of thousands of tenants by the Duke and Countess of Sutherland in the North Highlands. By 1850, sheep, having failed to be as profitable as hoped, were replaced by deer, and in 1886 the remaining tenants were given secure tenancy of their land through the Crofters Act. The Clearances were not the only factor in a century of depopulation and decline for the Highlands and Islands, but in an era where the Highland landscape became the romantic image of Scotland, by the end of the Clearances there were few Highland people left to clutter the view.

The Northeast

The city of Aberdeen, the third largest in Scotland today, became a royal burgh in the 12th century. Founded between the rivers Dee and Don, Aberdeen is known as 'the Granite City' after its local grey granite architecture. Aberdeen grew as the main seaport and trading centre of the northeast, with a distinctive cultural and economic history. In the 19th century, shipbuilding and fishing were the main industries of the city, while the rich farming lands of Aberdeenshire saw the breeding of Aberdeen Angus beef cattle. In 1848, Queen Victoria and her husband Prince Albert made their first visit to Aberdeenshire, and in 1852 Albert bought Balmoral Castle and the surrounding estate. After centuries of neglect, this was the beginning of a new relationship between Scotland and the monarchy, with Victoria's residencies at Balmoral inspiring an influx of the British upper classes, and fishing and the hunting and shooting of game (rather than Highlanders) becoming the principal industry of the rural Highland economy. Balmoral remains a private residence of the British royal family, who spend every August in an area that through this historic association is known as Royal Deeside.

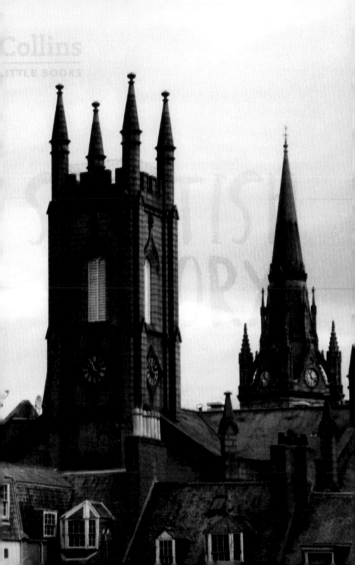

Whisky

The name 'whisky' derives from the Gaelic 'uisge beatha', meaning 'water of life'. The origins of distilling malted barley and water are unknown, but the first recorded mention of whisky is in 1494, when James IV placed an official crown order. Until the Reformation, monasteries were the main producers of whisky, but from 1560 until the early 19th century, whisky, faced by government restrictions and the disapproval of the Kirk, became a small-scale and illicit pleasure. The modern whisky industry began in the 19th century, with the easing of government taxation, improvements in the distilling process, and the development of blended whisky, which by mixing traditional malt whisky with grain whisky, produced a smoother taste. When French vineyards were decimated by blight in the 1880s, whisky producers saw the opportunity to export globally, particularly to the USA, where whisky was rebranded as 'Scotch', in order to differentiate from whisky made in other countries – a historically intriguing use of language, as other than with reference to whisky and in some recipes the term 'Scotch' is no longer considered an acceptable form of 'Scottish' or 'Scots'.

'Scotch whisky' is officially whisky matured in Scotland in oak casks for a minimum of three years. There are over 100 distilleries in Scotland, divided into five separate regions (Speyside, Highland, Lowland, the Hebridean island of Islay, and Campbeltown on the Kintyre peninsula). Speyside in the northeast is the largest region, with Dufftown the home of the two best-selling malt whiskies, Glenfiddich and Glenlivet. However, single malt whisky only makes up around 5% of total Scotch whisky sales, with blended whiskies dominating a £4 billion global industry. William Grant & Sons from Dufftown are the largest Scottish-owned whisky producer, but the legacy of the Scottish 'whisky barons' is seen in the iconic brands of Chivas Regal (created by the Chivas family in Speyside), Ballantine's (originally from Edinburgh), and – the most successful of all – Johnnie Walker. Launched by the Walker family of Kilmarnock in 1909, Johnnie Walker Red and Black Labels sell over 18 million cases a year, making the image of the Johnnie Walker 'striding man' – apparently modelled on the firm's eponymous founder – arguably the most recognized Scot in the world.

Medicine

In parallel to the Enlightenment flourishing of science and the arts, the 18th century was also the beginning of a golden age in Scottish medicine. The founding of the Edinburgh Medical School and the Glasgow School of Medicine, in 1726 and 1751 respectively, saw Scotland at the cutting edge of medical surgery and research, with Scottish-trained doctors practising all over the world. Scientific innovation was at the heart of Scottish medical excellence: in Edinburgh in 1847 obstetrician James Young Simpson became the first physician in the world to use anaesthesia successfully in childbirth, a development that would save countless millions of lives. English physician Joseph Lister also began his medical career in Edinburgh before transferring to the Glasgow Royal Infirmary, founded in 1797, as Professor of Surgery. In 1865, Lister became the first surgeon to pioneer the use of chemicals to treat wounds, kill germs, and reduce infections. Through sterilization Lister reduced fatalities, and antisepsis was eventually internationally adopted as standard practice, another great advance in medical history pioneered or, in the case of James Simpson, born in Scotland.

James Clerk Maxwell

Scotland's greatest scientist was born in Edinburgh, became Professor of Physics in Aberdeen, and spent much of his life at his family home in Galloway, before continuing his research in Cambridge, England. In 1861, James Clerk Maxwell demonstrated the world's first colour photograph (a tartan ribbon), but his true genius was in the fledgling field of electromagnetism. In the 1860s, Maxwell published a series of mathematical theories and equations, which culminated in 1864 with the establishment of the link between light and electricity. Maxwell correctly stated that the world we live in consists of electromagnetic radio waves all around us, but so revolutionary were his findings that it was not until 1887, and the physical discovery of radio waves, for his theories to be proven, so ushering in the modern understanding of the world. Maxwell did not live to see the vindication of his research, dying in 1879 at the age of only 48. However, while his extraordinary legacy is often overlooked in Scotland, internationally, the visionary James Clerk Maxwell is considered the greatest scientific mind of the 19th century, and one of the greatest there has ever been.

Inventors

With Watt's steam engine, Bell's telephone, Baird's television, and Fleming's discovery of penicillin, Scotland is renowned for its history of invention. However, there are numerous other, mostly neglected, Scottish inventors who have also changed the world. In 1787, Alexander Meikle invented a threshing machine for agriculture. In 1816, Robert Stirling invented the closed-cycle heat engine. In 1823, Charles Macintosh invented the eponymous 'Mackintosh' waterproof raincoat. In 1839, James Nasmyth invented the steam hammer, the first industrial machine. In 1840, Alexander Bain invented the electric clock, and still we only scratch the surface of Scottish ingenuity. More contentiously, Scotland lays claim to the invention of the bicycle in 1839, when Kirkpatrick Macmillan rode a pedal-driven, two-wheeled vehicle along the roads of Dumfriesshire. Sadly, Macmillan never patented his 'bicycle' and there is no historical confirmation of this reputed achievement. This oversight is perhaps compensated for by pneumatic tyres being invented, not once, but twice by two Scots; Robert Thomson in 1845, and more famously, John Boyd Dunlop in 1888.

Engineering

As the Industrial Revolution gathered momentum at the end of the 19th century, it was imperative that Scotland's transport network underwent its own revolution. In 1790, the Forth and Clyde Canal linked east and west Lowland Scotland together, and in 1822 the Caledonian Canal, designed by Thomas Telford, was completed, opening up the Highlands from Fort William to Inverness. Telford, the greatest civil engineer of his day, built so many bridges and roads in Britain that he was called 'the Colossus of Roads', but it was his Scottish contemporary John Loudon McAdam who had a greater global legacy, with his revolutionary process of building hard, smooth, long-lasting roads that became known as 'macadamization' (and, when tar was added, 'tarmac') in his honour. In the 19th century, Scottish engineers, with their reputation for excellence and ingenuity, were employed to build the infrastructure of the world. However, perhaps the greatest monument to Scottish engineering was completed over the Firth of Forth in 1890. This was William Arroll's Forth Bridge, linking Edinburgh to Fife, then the longest railway bridge in the world.

Industry

In the 19th century, Scotland's population doubled, growing to exceed four million, and for the first time more Scots lived in towns and cities than in the countryside. Glasgow, the self-proclaimed 'Second City of Empire', saw the greatest increase with a tenfold rise in population and reached one million in 1911. Glasgow was a world leader in shipbuilding and the manufacture of locomotives for the expanding railways. Throughout the Lowlands, however, industry fuelled the growth of urbanization in Scottish towns. Ayrshire, Lanarkshire, and Fife were at the heart of the coal industry, Motherwell the centre of Scottish steel, Falkirk a town famous for iron, and West Lothian the location for the shale oil industry, as pioneered by James Young, the inventor of paraffin in 1850. Dundee, Scotland's fourth-largest city today, flourished as the world's largest producer of jute goods, but also gained prominence through its association with marmalade, created by the Keiller family in 1797, and the publishing of popular newspapers, periodicals, and comics. This triumvirate of phonetically similar industries saw Dundee christened the city of 'the three Js' – jute, jam, and journalism.

Shipbuilding

In the 19th century the British Empire ruled the waves and it was Scottish shipbuilders who invariably built the warships, sailing ships, and ocean liners that criss-crossed the globe. Aberdeen, Dundee, and Leith were all major shipbuilding centres, but it was the Clyde shipyards of Glasgow, Dumbarton, Clydebank, and Port Glasgow that were the heart of Scottish shipbuilding. In 1869, the world-famous sailing ship, the *Cutty Sark*, was built in Dumbarton. However, it was steamships that were the future: in 1802, Alexander Symington built one of the world's first steamboats; in 1838, the *Sirius* became the first steamship to cross the Atlantic; and in 1842, Robert Napier, co-founder of the Cunard Line, built the first modern shipyard in Glasgow. By the end of the 19th century, Scots ran many of the world's great shipping companies – Cunard, P & O, Castle, Allan, and the British-Indian – and the Clyde was the premier shipbuilding region in the world. Scottish shipbuilding slowly declined through the 20th century to the point where only two major shipyards remain today. However, these still retain the noble heritage of when 20% of all the shipping in the world was 'Clydebuilt'.

Emigration

Despite the doubling of the Scottish population in the 19th century, two million Scots left their homeland. The British Empire gave Scots the opportunity to seek a better life in the colonies, although the USA remained for most the ultimate destination. As the USA expanded, Scots ventured westwards from their 18th-century heartlands of the Carolinas across the continent to the Pacific coast. In Chicago in 1850, Allan Pinkerton founded the famous detective agency that originated the phrase 'private eye'. In Detroit in 1903, David Dunbar Buick founded the Buick automobile company. Meanwhile, in California, during a lifetime espousing environmentalism and the protection of natural wilderness, John Muir led the campaign that established Yosemite National Park in 1890. Most financially successful of all the Scottish migrants was Andrew Carnegie from Dunfermline, who in Pittsburgh made such a fortune from steel that he became both the world's wealthiest man and the world's most generous philanthropist. Carnegie established libraries and charities across America, but did not forget where he came from and was also a benefactor to the Fife town that he left when he was only 13.

Canada

At the end of the American War of Independence in 1783, Britain retained control of the land to the north, and it was Scots who played a pivotal role in the history of the country that we know today as Canada. The longest river in Canada, the Mackenzie, is named after explorer Alexander Mackenzie. The city of Calgary is named after a small village in Mull. Scots ran the mighty fur trading companies around the Hudson Bay that dominated the early economy, and also built the Canadian Pacific Railway that linked the country together in 1885. So many Scots from the Highlands and Islands emigrated there that, until the 20th century, Canada became the only country outside Scotland where Gaelic was widely spoken, and when the movement for Canadian self-government and Confederation grew in the mid-19th century it was Scots who were inevitably at the fore. In 1867, Canada became a federal nation, and it was appropriate that its first prime minister, John A Macdonald, who served in that role for 19 years, hailed from Glasgow, the most illustrious of all the Scots who built a new country thousands of miles from home.

Australia

Around the world perhaps only Australia can equal
Canada for historic Scottish influence: the city of Perth
was named after its Scottish equivalent; Brisbane, the
state capital of Queensland, takes the name of Scottish
administrator Thomas Brisbane; while Andrew Fisher
from Ayrshire was three times Australian prime minister
between 1908 and 1916. The national anthem, 'Advance
Australia Fair', was written by Peter Dodds McCormick
in 1878, while a rather different genre of musical
anthem is composed by the rock band AC/DC, founded
in 1973 by Malcolm and Angus Young, originally from
Glasgow. However, the Scot with the most enduring
legacy was Lachlan Macquarie, from the island of Ulva,
who served as Governor-General of New South Wales
between 1809 and 1822. Before Macquarie, Australia was
a small prison colony, but under his governorship,
convicts were rehabilitated, Sydney became a city, and
thousands of law-abiding settlers arrived, beginning the
British colonization of the Australian continent. For his
colonial initiatives Macquarie is often given the title of
'Father of Australia', even if this honour somewhat
neglects the thousands of years of Australian history
that went before.

Asia

Scotland's embracing of the British Empire is best exemplified by its long-standing relationship with the continent of Asia. Dundee prospered through importing raw jute from India and turning it into sacks. Paisley became renowned for the 'Paisley pattern' that originated in Kashmir. In China, Scottish merchants William Jardine and James Matheson founded a business empire, initially predicated on the opium trade, which led to the colonization (in 1842) and growth of a small Chinese island by the name of Hong Kong. The Hong Kong and Shanghai Banking Corporation (HSBC) was founded by another Scot, Thomas Sutherland, in 1865. In Japan, Thomas Glover, 'the Scottish Samurai', played a crucial role in the country's re-engagement with the West and industrialization in the late 19th century. However, it was Britain's obsession with tea that best exemplified Scottish mercantile acumen. In the 19th century, Scots had established the first tea plantations in India and Ceylon (now Sri Lanka), and in 1890 Thomas Lipton from Glasgow launched his global brand of Lipton's, so ensuring that perhaps even more than whisky, it is tea that is Scotland's national drink.

Banking

Scotland's first great inventor was mathematician John Napier, who in 1614 invented logarithms and popularized the decimal point. Napier was the first numerate Scot to be internationally recognized, but subsequently it was in the financial world where Scots became prominent, with the central banks of the UK and France, the Bank of England and the Banque de France, being founded by William Paterson and John Law, in 1694 and 1716 respectively. In Scotland, the Bank of England is also the central bank. However, three retail banks – the Bank of Scotland, the Royal Bank of Scotland (RBS), and the Clydesdale Bank – have the legal right to print their own sterling banknotes, which should be universally accepted throughout the UK, even if in practice this does not always prove to be the case. Edinburgh is the historic financial centre of Scotland, and the birthplace of the Royal Bank of Scotland in 1727. However, with the Bank of Scotland and the Clydesdale Bank both now subsidiaries of non-Scottish banking groups, and RBS being majority-owned by the UK government since the banking crash of 2008, there are currently no major Scottish-owned banks.

Alexander Graham Bell

In Boston, Massachusetts, in 1876, a professor of vocal physiology uttered the words 'Mr Watson, come here, I want to see you', so successfully making the world's first telephone call. The man who spoke was Alexander Graham Bell, who was born in Edinburgh in 1847. The Bell family left Scotland in 1867, and in 1871 Alexander moved to the USA, where he found work as a teacher of the deaf. In 1877, with his patent for the telephone successfully accepted, Bell founded the Bell Telephone Company, which, as AT&T, using the Bell System, became the largest telephone company in the world. Despite historical controversy concerning the intellectual legitimacy of his patent, Bell overcame all legal objections, and in 1880 founded Bell Labs in New Jersey, the leading scientific research institution of the 20th century. Bell continued to invent and innovate until his death in Nova Scotia, Canada, in 1922, but it is as the inventor of the telephone, the greatest advance in communications in modern history, that he is remembered. Somewhat ironically, Bell demonstrated a not untypical Scottish male reluctance to speak on the phone, and rarely, if ever, found the necessity to give someone 'a bell'.

Golf

Golf (originally called 'gowf') has been played on the east coast of Scotland since at least the 14th century. James IV, Mary, Queen of Scots, and Charles I were all early players, but the history of modern golf begins with the formation of the Gentlemen Golfers of Edinburgh in 1744, who played on Leith Links and drafted the first thirteen *Rules of Play*, many of which remain unaltered today. The first record of golf in St Andrews was in 1506, and the Society of St Andrews Golfers (later the Royal & Ancient) was founded in 1754. In the 19th century, the Old Course at St Andrews, under the guidance of golf's most influential figure, 'Old' Tom Morris, became recognized as the 'Home of Golf'. The first Open Championship was held at Prestwick in Ayrshire in 1860, with the traditional Claret Jug first presented to the winner in 1872. In the late 19th century, golf was adopted by both England and America, with Scots founding the USA's oldest club, St Andrew's, in 1888. Over the next 25 years Scottish golfers successfully converted America into a giant driving range, but by 1914 the students had overtaken their teachers and golf was no longer a Scottish game, but an international sport.

Football

In 1871, the first ever rugby football international was held in Edinburgh between Scotland and England, and in 1872 the same two countries met on a cricket pitch in Glasgow to play the first ever association football international. In 1873, Scotland founded its own rugby and football associations, so establishing their sporting national independence, and in the 19th century Scotland was the leading football nation in Britain, and therefore the world. When English football turned professional in 1885, Scottish players – known as 'the Scotch Professors' on account of their revolutionary passing game that became the template of the modern game – were recruited to the leading English clubs. Preston North End became the first English League champions in 1889 with a majority of Scots in their side, while in 1895 Sunderland won the League with an entirely Scottish first XI. Queen's Park from Glasgow was the first Scottish club in 1867, but after the Scottish League was formed in 1890, the club was supplanted by its Glasgow rivals Rangers (founded in 1875) and Celtic (founded in 1888), who soon established an enduring domestic duopoly on Scotland's national team sport.

Literature

In the 18th century, Robert Burns wrote in Scots, but by the end of 19th century, English, the language of education, law, the Kirk, and the state, had replaced Scots as the language of Scottish literature, with Gaelic reduced to fewer than 250,000 speakers and continuing to fall. The *Encyclopaedia Britannica* was published in Edinburgh from 1768 to 1901; William Collins published bibles and dictionaries in Glasgow, and James Murray worked for 36 years on the *Oxford English Dictionary*, published in 1928. In 1883, Robert Louis Stevenson, from the renowned Stevenson family of lighthouse builders, wrote his classic story of pirates, *Treasure Island*, and the Jacobite adventure, *Kidnapped*, in 1886, while in 1904 and 1908, JM (James Matthew) Barrie and Kenneth Grahame enchanted readers with their tales of Neverland and Toad Hall in *Peter Pan* and *The Wind in the Willows*. Stevenson, Barrie, and Grahame all left Scotland, the archetypal Scots away from home, and in 1886, it was Stevenson who created the iconic literary representation of a shared and divided personality in *The Strange Case of Dr Jekyll & Mr Hyde*.

Law and order

After the Act of Union of 1707, Scotland retained its separate legal system. The High Court of the Judiciary tries the most serious criminal cases, while the Court of Session is the highest civil court and sits in Parliament House in Edinburgh, the former home of the first Scottish Parliament. Local cases are judged by sheriffs, while procurator fiscals determine whether a case should go to trial. In Scots law there are uniquely three possible verdicts in a trial, with the retention of the rarely used ancient verdict of 'not proven' as a controversial alternative to the more familiar 'not guilty'. In 1887, the world's famous fictional criminologist, Sherlock Holmes, was created by Edinburgh-born Arthur Conan Doyle and inspired by his university lecturer Joseph Bell. Over the next forty years, the fictional Holmes, following the traditional Scottish Enlightenment virtues of reason and deduction, solved countless crimes and mysteries that baffled Scotland Yard, the alternative name for the London police force. Sadly, the real Scotland Yard had no actual Scottish origins, but were so named for the elementary reason that Scotland Yard was the address of their headquarters.

Immigration

In the mid-19th century, 1,400 years after Irish invaders had created the kingdom of Dalriada, a new influx of Irish people arrived in the cities of industrial Scotland to escape famine and poverty. By 1851, 20% of the population of Glasgow and Dundee were Irish-born, and as the majority of these were Catholic, for the first time since the Reformation Scotland had a significant non-Protestant minority. The Irish immigrants initially lived in the poorest areas of Scotland's cities and endured discrimination and prejudice, with the religious divide creating long-standing sectarian tension, particularly in the West of Scotland. The football clubs of Hibernian in Edinburgh, founded in 1875, and Celtic in Glasgow, founded in 1888, are both named in honour of their Irish origins, and the ultimately successful integration of the Irish into Scottish society was the forerunner of subsequent smaller influxes of immigrants in the 20th and 21st centuries. Today, significant Italian, Pakistani, and Polish communities, not forgetting the largest minority of all, the English, all call Scotland home, so continuing Scotland's long history of supporting a diverse and multi-ethnic population.

Home Rule

In the 18th century, the Kirk was for most Scots the principal institution in their everyday lives, both spiritually and through the administration of education and poor relief. However, with the urbanization of the 19th century, and a Kirk diminished by decades of internal divisions, local government was reformed with the creation of county councils in 1889. Nationally, the Scottish Office was established in 1885, but was located in London, and while the 19th century saw the enfranchisement of the Scottish male population, they elected to vote for the major British parties, the Liberals and the Conservatives. Britain had already conceded self-government status to Canada and Australia, and in the 1880s, the Liberals proposed Home Rule for Ireland, with Scotland added as an afterthought. The Scottish Home Rule Association was founded in 1886, but was politically overshadowed by the question of Ireland. In 1913, the Government of Scotland bill finally came before Parliament. The bill failed. However, there was widespread public support in Scotland for Home Rule, and when Irish Home Rule passed in 1914, it seemed only a matter of time before the Scots would follow suit.

Prime ministers

In the 300 years since 1707, Scots have shown an increasing inclination to attain the political power unavailable to them in Scotland itself. John A Macdonald was the very first prime minister of Canada in 1867, Andrew Fisher was three times prime minister of Australia between 1908 and 1916, and Peter Fraser was prime minister of New Zealand from 1940 to 1949. The first Scots-born prime minister of Britain was the Earl of Bute in 1762–3, followed by the Earl of Aberdeen in 1852–5, and Arthur Balfour in 1902–5. The first Scots-born prime minister to represent a Scottish constituency and win a UK general election was Henry Campbell-Bannerman from Glasgow. Campbell-Bannerman led the Liberals to a landslide victory in 1906 and initiated a programme of social reforms before his untimely death in 1908. There have been three subsequent British prime ministers born in Scotland, all, at least initially, representing the Labour Party: Ramsay MacDonald was twice prime minister between 1924 and 1935; Gordon Brown held the post between 2007 and 2010; while the longest-serving Scots-born prime minister was Tony Blair, who served from 1997 to 2007.

The Labour Party

From the mid-19th century until the 1920s the Liberals were the dominant party in Scottish politics, with four-times British prime minister William Gladstone serving as MP for Midlothian. After their British general election victory of 1906, the Liberals were proponents of social and political reform, which included legislation for Scottish Home Rule, policies that were in part influenced by a new political party with whom they had in 1906 briefly joined in electoral alliance. In 1888, James Keir Hardie, a former miner and trade unionist from Ayrshire, had founded the Scottish Labour Party as a working-class socialist movement. Moving to England, Hardie became an MP in 1892, and in 1900 brought the growing trade union movement and various socialist groupings together to found the Labour Party. Hardie became the first parliamentary leader of the Labour Party in 1906, and such was the Scottish influence on the rising party that he was the first of five successive Scots-born leaders, culminating in Ramsay MacDonald, who in 1924 became their first prime minister, as Labour replaced the Liberals as one of the two major political parties in Scotland, as well as Britain.

The Great War

The First World War between 1914 and 1918 had a profound effect on the history of Scotland. The British Navy was based at Scapa Flow in Orkney, where in 1919 the defeated German equivalent scuttled its own fleet. British troops were armed with the Lee-Enfield rifle – named after its Scots-born designer, James Lee – while the industrial Lowlands produced munitions, ships, and fuel for the war effort, which required the employment of over 200,000 Scottish women in the wartime factories. Throughout Scotland young men volunteered to fight in a conflict that was supposed to be over by Christmas, but dragged on for four years in the trenches of France and Flanders. The British army was led by Douglas Haig from Edinburgh, whose controversial strategy of a war of attrition proved ultimately successful, but at the cost of an unparalleled loss of life. By the time the guns were silenced in November 1918, 220,000 Scots had been either killed or wounded, by far the highest number of casualties Scotland has suffered in any conflict in its history.

Red Clydeside

Scottish Home Rule, which had seemed so inevitable in 1914, slowly faded from political view after 1918. The First World War saw strikes on Clydeside in protest against poor working and housing conditions, and in 1919, a massive demonstration in George Square, Glasgow, with the red flag of socialism prominently displayed, panicked the government so much that it employed the army in response. There was no revolution in Scotland, but in 1922 the Labour Party for the first time gained the most MPs in Scotland, so creating a new political landscape in which Labour and the Conservatives divided Scotland between them. The Scottish National Party was founded in 1934, but initially made minimal political impact. The Depression of the 1930s, unemployment, the decline of Scotland's traditional industrial base, and the impending catastrophe in Europe were the overriding issues of the interwar years, with constitutional change no longer on the agenda. Labour finally won a landslide general election victory in 1945, justifying the party's long gradual march to electoral success, and in Scotland a vindication for the legend and socialist legacy of 'Red Clydeside'.

Radio and television

In 1922, the British Broadcasting Company was founded in London to broadcast radio programmes to the nation and appointed John Reith from Stonehaven to run the fledgling company. Reith remained in charge of the BBC until 1938, by which time it had been renamed the British Broadcasting Corporation and, following Reith's original mission statement of 'inform, educate, and entertain', established the template for public broadcasting that we know today. In 1936, during Reith's tenure as the BBC's first director-general, and despite the austere Scot's personal antipathy, the BBC began broadcasting television programmes. This medium had been invented only ten years before, in January 1926, when John Logie Baird, an engineer and inventor from Helensburgh, made the world's first public demonstration of 'wireless with pictures'. Baird made the first demonstration of colour television in 1928, the first official BBC broadcast in 1936, and despite being overtaken by rival systems he continued to innovate until his death in 1946, sadly not living to see his invention become the dominant medium of the post-war world.

Alexander Fleming

The first Scot to win the Nobel Prize for Medicine was John James Richard Macleod, a professor of physiology from Perthshire, who led the team in Toronto that isolated insulin in 1921. Macleod won his Nobel Prize in 1923 as the overseer of this life-changing medical breakthrough, but five years later, the greatest medical advance of the 20th century was brought about by a happy accident. Alexander Fleming was a farmer's son from near Darvel in East Ayrshire, who moved to London to qualify as a surgeon. Fleming's speciality was bacteriology and in 1928, after returning from holiday, he discovered that a natural antibiotic substance had grown on a bacterial culture that had been left exposed while he was away. Fleming named this mould 'penicillin', but the revolutionary importance of his discovery was not developed until the 1940s, when penicillin was successfully mass-produced and became the most important life-saving drug the world had ever seen. Fleming received the Nobel Prize in 1945, but the true legacy for this modest bacteriologist was the millions of people who owed their lives to a forgetful Scotsman who didn't tidy up properly.

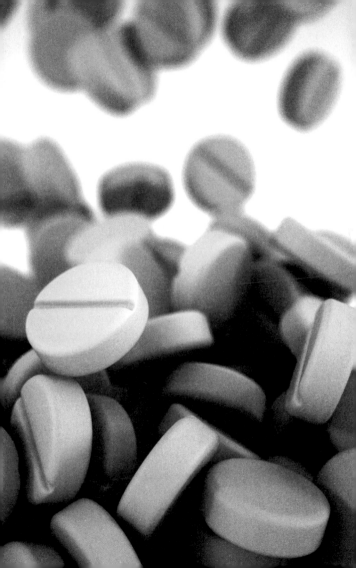

Loch Ness

For the majority of the visitors who arrive in Scotland every year there is one destination that must be seen above all other – Loch Ness. Scotland's largest loch (Gaelic for 'lake') by surface area is Loch Lomond, a popular tourist destination since the 19th century. However, Loch Ness is deeper and holds a greater volume of water than its southern rival, and it was this very depth that caused an international sensation in 1933. The earliest record of a mysterious sea-creature living in the loch dates back to AD 565, when it was said that St Columba encountered a fearsome beast. For the next 1,400 years the loch remained relatively calm until a spate of sightings captured the public's imagination, with an iconic photo purportedly taken by a respected surgeon in 1934 offering credible evidence that the 'Loch Ness Monster' did exist. There have been numerous further sightings of 'Nessie' since 1934, but extensive searches of the loch have yet to locate the reclusive creature, and the 'Surgeon's Photo' was finally exposed as a hoax in 1975. However, such setbacks do not appear to have detracted from the world's fascination with what might just possibly lie beneath the water.

World War II

Compared to the carnage of the First World War, Scotland statistically suffered fewer casualties in the Second World War. Nevertheless, 58,000 Scots lost their lives between 1939 and 1945, and the horror of war was brought directly to Scotland's door with 6,000 killed by enemy bombing, with the town of Clydebank almost completely destroyed in 1941. Strategically, Scotland played a crucial role in the conflict, with the merchant navy and Scottish naval bases maintaining the North Atlantic and Arctic sea routes, while thousands of commandos were trained at their headquarters in Lochaber and the D-Day landings were rehearsed along the Scottish coastline. In the Battle of Britain of 1940, the employment of radar, developed by Robert Watson-Watt, proved crucial to British survival in the country's darkest days. Moreover, this was a conflict that involved the entire Scottish population. Scottish men and women served in the armed forces overseas, in the factories, in the mines, and on the land at home for six long years before victory was finally achieved in 1945.

Festivals

The Scots name for New Year's Eve is 'Hogmanay', an obscure word possibly derived from the Old French 'aguillanneuf', meaning 'New Year's Eve gift'. Due to the Kirk's historic Calvinist disapproval of the pre-Reformation celebration of Christmas, New Year has until recently been the principal Scottish winter festival, with Christmas Day only made a public holiday in Scotland in 1958. Scotland's take on the New Year festivities has been successfully exported around the world and Hogmanay remains a major festival in Scotland, where it is fair to say that 'drink may be taken'. Scotland's largest annual festivities, however, are held in Edinburgh every August. The first Edinburgh International Festival took place in 1947, with the Edinburgh Festival Fringe (originally outside or 'on the fringe' of the official Festival) beginning in 1948. The Fringe has overtaken the International Festival and is now by far the larger of the two: with over 2,500 different shows it is the largest annual arts festival in the world. However, with the Military Tattoo and the Edinburgh Book Festival all held at the same time, visitors and locals alike tend not to differentiate between the different elements of 'the Festival'.

North Sea oil

Scotland has a long history as a pioneer in both oil and gas. In 1792, William Murdock invented gas lighting, while James Young, the inventor of paraffin, opened the world's first oil refinery in Bathgate in 1850. Over a century later, in 1969, oil and gas were discovered underneath the North Sea, and when further fields were found east of Shetland and Aberdeen in the 1970s it sparked an oil boom in the northeast of Scotland. Aberdeen became the onshore centre of North Sea oil, bringing new prosperity to the city and the region. Shetland, Scotland's most northerly islands, which was previously best known for fishing and its diminutive ponies, also played a part with the giant Sullom Voe oil terminal becoming operational in 1978. Production of the black gold began in 1975, and by 1984 the North Sea had made Britain the fifth-largest oil producer in the world, with production levels reaching a peak at the end of the millennium. With decades of reserves left, and new fields being developed west of Shetland, North Sea oil is today an integral part of the country's economy. The question that has been asked in Scotland ever since 1969, however, is which country does the oil belong to?

Nationalism

By the 1970s the Scottish economy was in decline. The end of the British Empire had reduced Scottish markets, and attempts to diversify had failed to change Scotland's reliance on the struggling traditional heavy industries of coal, steel, and shipbuilding. Post-war nationalization, consumerism, new housing (with the worst pre-war slums demolished), and the development of New Towns gave protection to the economy and saw standards of living rise, but with unemployment and inflation both increasing and the discovery of oil fuelling a constitutional debate, the Scottish National Party (SNP) made an electoral breakthrough in 1974, winning 11 seats. In response to this nationalist upsurge, the Labour government resurrected the concept of Scottish Home Rule, last seen in 1913, and proposed a new Scottish assembly in Edinburgh, with limited devolved legislative powers, but only if 40% of the Scottish electorate agreed. In March 1979, a referendum was held, with 33% voting in favour, 31% voting against, but crucially 36% didn't vote at all. So, for the second time, Scottish devolution was abandoned before it even began.

Sport

For a small nation Scotland has achieved considerable sporting success. In football, Celtic won the European Cup in 1967, Scottish managers Matt Busby and Bill Shankly are synonymous with Manchester United and Liverpool respectively, while Alex Ferguson became the most successful manager ever in English football. In motor racing, Jim Clark and Jackie Stewart became multiple Formula One world champions. In cycling, Chris Hoy won six Olympic gold medals. In tennis, Andy Murray won the US Open and Wimbledon titles. Even in baseball, Glasgow-born Bobby Thomson entered American sporting folklore in 1951, when he hit the most famous home run in the sport's history. In Scotland itself, St Andrews, Muirfield in East Lothian, Carnoustie in Angus, and Troon and Turnberry in Ayrshire host the Open (never the 'British Open') Championship, and Murrayfield in Edinburgh has been the home of Scottish rugby union since 1925. Hampden Park in Glasgow, built in 1903, was the largest football stadium in the world until 1950, with a record attendance of 150,000 in 1937. Football remains Scotland's national sport, with the national team's independence fiercely protected regardless of diminishing performances on the pitch.

Film and culture

In 1962, Sean Connery from Edinburgh first appeared as James Bond in *Dr No*, so beginning the modern cultural image of Scots as strong, self-deprecating, and cool, both patriotic and international. The historic tartan image has been reinvented for a global market, but with a distinctive new accent. Since 1962, Scotland has provided the iconic cinematic locations for *Brave*, Eilean Donan Castle in Lochalsh for *Highlander*, Edinburgh for *Trainspotting*, Rosslyn Chapel in Midlothian for *The Da Vinci Code*, and the Glenfinnan Viaduct in Lochaber for the *Harry Potter* series. The 1995 film *Braveheart* was mostly filmed in Ireland, but reignited interest in the Stirling area, and nearby Doune Castle has become internationally famous for appearing in the *Outlander* television series. Despite concerted efforts to support Scotland's other national language, only 1% of the population speak Gaelic. But in film, music, and video games, where Edinburgh's Rockstar North produce the hugely successful *Grand Theft Auto* franchise, Scottish voices and creative talent have never been so globally popular. In 2012, fifty years after Connery's debut as Bond, the climax of *Skyfall* was set in Glencoe, a fitting anniversary for an era where Scottish culture was both shaken and stirred.

Devolution

Between 1979 and 1997 the Conservatives held power in Britain. The Conservatives were previously the traditional electoral choice of Scotland's middle classes, but after 1979 they became increasingly unpopular as their economic policies saw high unemployment and the end of Scotland's traditional industries of coal and steel. The policies of Margaret Thatcher, prime minister from 1979 to 1990, saw growth in the housing market and in financial services, but her staunch Unionism and abandonment of Scotland's industrial base was perceived as anti-Scottish, and all of the Scottish Conservative MPs lost their seats in 1997. Labour was the dominant party in Scotland from 1979 to 1997, and supported Scottish devolution as a means to assuage the democratic deficit brought about by Scotland being ruled by a party which had little support within the country. In September 1997, the new Labour government called a new referendum for the establishment of a Scottish Parliament with greater powers than the assembly proposed in 1979. The Scottish people voted overwhelmingly 75% to 25% in favour, a result that incidentally also surpassed the 40% threshold set 18 years before.

Dolly and the Higgs boson

In 1958, the development of ultrasound pregnancy scans at Glasgow University was another example of a life-changing advance in science originating in Scotland. However, in 1997 Scotland truly shocked the world when the Roslin Institute, an animal research institution in Midlothian, announced the first successful cloning of a mammal. The mammal was a lamb, cloned from a cell taken from the mammary gland of a living sheep, and she was named Dolly in honour of the singer Dolly Parton. Dolly lived, or relived, in Roslin until her death in 2003, and gave birth to six healthy lambs, none of whom were called Jolene. The moral implications of Dolly, who is now on display at the National Museum of Scotland, for the future of mankind are uncertain, but in 2013 Scotland was at the forefront of another momentous scientific event. The Higgs boson was named after the University of Edinburgh's Professor Peter Higgs, who had first predicted the existence of this elementary particle in 1964. For nearly fifty years, the search for the Higgs boson became the Holy Grail of science, until it was discovered (probably) in 2013 at the Large Hadron Collider in Switzerland.

Holyrood

On the 1st of July 1999, Scotland's first parliament in 292 years was opened at the Assembly Hall of the Church of Scotland in Edinburgh, before moving to a new, highly controversial, home opposite the Palace of Holyroodhouse in 2004. The Holyrood parliament's responsibilities include health, education, justice, transport, culture, the environment, and rural affairs, with taxation, welfare, defence, and foreign affairs remaining the responsibility of Westminster. There are 129 Members of the Scottish Parliament (MSPs), 56 of whom are elected on a 'party list' basis to ensure seats are awarded in proportion to the votes cast for each party. The headquarters of the Scottish Government (formerly Executive) are located at St Andrew's House in Edinburgh, the former home of the Scottish Office, which ran Scotland on behalf of the British government until 1999. The leader of the Scottish Government is known as the First Minister, with Labour's Donald Dewar, a long-standing advocate of devolution, the very first First Minister in 1999. The Labour Party formed the Scottish government, in coalition with the Liberal Democrats, and remained in power until 2007.

Referendum 2014

In 2007, for the first time since 1707, a nationalist government was formed in Scotland. After their initial success in the 1970s, the SNP had become the main opposition party in 1999, and in 2007 won the Scottish election with just one more seat than Labour. Their leader, Alex Salmond, became First Minister of a minority administration and at the 2011 Scottish election won an overall majority in parliament, enabling the SNP, with the agreement of the UK government, to hold a national referendum on Scotland's constitutional future. A date of the 18th of September 2014 was announced for a referendum, and the Scottish people were to be asked 'Should Scotland be an independent country?' Opinion polls had shown a clear majority of Scots preferring to remain within the UK, but the margins had narrowed dramatically, until with the world watching, and Scotland undergoing unprecedented political debate, 85% of the electorate went to the polls. In the final count 45% of Scots voted 'Yes' to becoming an independent country, however 55% voted 'No', and the constitutional status quo was confirmed.

Post referendum

After losing the 2014 referendum, SNP First Minister Alex Salmond resigned and was succeeded by his deputy, Nicola Sturgeon, Scotland's first female First Minister. However, despite their setback, it was the SNP who became the political beneficiaries of a Scotland that had become divided by the referendum along Nationalist and Unionist lines. In the 2015 UK general election the SNP won an unparalleled 56 out of 59 seats, and in the 2016 Scottish election were returned to power for a third term. 2016 also saw the UK referendum on membership of the European Union, but while the UK narrowly voted to leave the EU, in Scotland the vote was 62% to 38% in favour of Remain. In March 2017, the Scottish Parliament voted in favour of calling another vote on Scottish independence before withdrawal from the EU, to decide Scotland's constitutional future once and for all. Yet with the UK government resistant to such a plebiscite, as has always has been the case in the history of Scotland, nobody knows for certain how the story will end.

Conclusion

In March 1707, with the Articles of Union passed by both the Scottish and English Parliaments and having received the royal assent of Queen Anne, James Ogilvy, the Earl of Seafield, Lord Chancellor of Scotland, and a supporter of Union, was heard to remark 'there's an end to an auld sang'. With these words Scotland ceased to be an independent nation. In retrospect, it was remarkable that Scotland (and previously Alba and the kingdoms of the Picts) had survived for so many centuries as varying invaders sought to unite the island of Britain. However, with the dissolution of the Scottish Parliament in 1707, the Earl of Seafield's observation – regardless of what the Scottish people thought about the Union – appeared an appropriate summary of a nation that had run its course and was about to be assimilated into a greater British entity.

Yet, as we have seen, the next 300 years saw the re-invention of Scotland as a country. It retained a separate identity and embraced a distinct national

culture and heritage, albeit one that was often more imagined than inherited. At the same time, the Scottish people, one step removed from political power at home, established an extraordinary legacy of scientific, academic, and economic achievement around the globe, and in the process created much of the world we know today.

In 1999, after a gap of 292 years, a new Scottish Parliament was opened in Edinburgh. It remains to be seen to what extent the history of Scotland will be changed by this return of political power. However, whether Holyrood continues as a devolved parliament within the United Kingdom, or is to become a parliament for an independent nation, the one thing that can be said with any certainty is that with hindsight the Earl of Seafield was wrong, and the 'auld sang' of Scottish history can still be heard today.

Index

A

Aberdeen 55, 60, 144, 160
Abernethy 38
Act of Union, 1707 5, 104, 108, 116,
    134, 178, 214
'Alba' 5, 14, 22, 24, 32, 34, 38, 106, 214
Albert, Prince 144
Alexander III 44, 46, 48
America 84, 116, 121, 140, 142
American War of Independence
    116, 140, 164
Andrew, St 18, 42
Anne, Queen 96, 102, 108, 214
Antonine Wall 11
Arbroath, Declaration of 58
Asia 166
'Auld Alliance' 72, 74
Australia 165, 184

B

bagpipes 58, 136
Baird, JL 154, 190
Balmoral Castle 144
banking 168
Bannockburn 4, 20, 52, 54, 55, 56
Barrie, JM 176
BBC 190
Bell, AG 154, 170
Bishops' Wars 86
Borders, the 66, 106, 142
British Army 187
Burns, Robert 5, 56, 124, 126, 176

C

Calanais (Callanish) 10
'Caledonia' 4, 11, 12
Calvin, John 80
Campbells 99
Canada 30, 164, 165, 184
Carnegie, Andrew 162
Catholic Church 33, 76, 77, 80, 98,
    102
Celtic tribes 11, 12
Charles I 86, 88, 92, 172
Charles II 92, 94
Charlie, Bonnie Prince 110, 112
Christianity 16, 18, 20, 76
Church of Scotland 33, 76, 80, 86,
    92, 94, 98, 120, 182, 210
clans 4, 68, 98, 99, 110, 112, 114, 132,
    134, 143
cloning 209
Clydebank 160, 196
Clydeside, 'Red' 188
Columba, St 20, 194
Conservatives 182, 188, 208
Constantine II 38
cotton 140, 142
Covenanters 86, 88, 94
Cromwell, Oliver 92
Culloden 4, 112, 114, 130, 132
Cumberland, Duke of 114
Cumbric language 30, 34, 36

D

Dalriada 14, 24, 180
Darien Scheme 100, 102
David I 40, 72
David II 62, 64
devolution 202, 208, 210–11
Dewar, Donald 210
diet 126
Dolly the sheep 209
Doyle, Arthur Conan 178
Duncan I 32
Dundee 55, 158, 160, 166, 180
Dunfermline 33, 54, 86

E

Edinburgh 5, 34, 46, 55, 76, 90, 94, 98, 110, 118, 130, 140, 150, 152, 156, 170, 172, 174, 202, 215
Edinburgh Castle 24, 34, 78
Edinburgh Festival 198
Edinburgh's New Town 122
Edinburgh, University of 60, 209
Edward the Elder 38
Edward I 24, 44, 48, 50, 52, 72
Edward II 52, 54
Edward VI 74
Edwin 34
electromagnetism 152
Elizabeth I 82
emigration 100, 114, 116, 162
engineering 156
English Civil Wars 86, 88, 92
English influence 40
Enlightenment 6, 118, 120, 121, 122, 150, 178
Episcopalians 94, 98

F

festivals 28, 198
feudal system 40
film and culture 206
First World War 187, 188, 196
Fisher, Andrew 165, 184
flags 18, 42, 84
Fleming, Alexander 154, 192
Flodden 70, 72
'Flower of Scotland' 56
football 174, 180, 204
France 72, 74, 77, 108
François II 74, 77

G

Gaelic 14, 22, 30, 98, 106, 114, 164, 176, 206
'Gaidhealtachd' 106
George I 108
George II 114
George III 122
George IV 122, 130, 132
Glasgow 36, 55, 121, 140, 150, 158, 160, 164–6, 180
Glasgow University 60, 138, 209
Glencoe Massacre 99
golf 172
Grahame, Kenneth 176

H

Hadrian's Wall 11
haggis 126
Hanoverians 102, 108
Hardie, James Keir 186
Hebrides 5, 26, 44, 46, 68, 70
Henry VIII 70, 74

'heritable jurisdictions' 98, 114
Higgs, Professor Peter 209
Higgs boson 209
'Highland Clearances' 143
Highlanders 5, 110, 112, 114, 118,
    128, 132, 134
Highlands 98, 99, 106, 108, 128,
    130, 156
Hogmanay 124, 198
Holyrood 210, 215
Home Rule 182, 186, 188, 202
Hume, David 118, 120, 121
Hutton, James 118, 120, 121

I
immigration 180
independence 54–6, 58, 62, 90,
    211–2
Industrial Revolution 6, 138, 140, 156
industry 158, 160, 187–8, 202
infrastructure 156
invention 154, 170, 190, 192, 200, 209
Iona 20
Ireland 84, 180, 182

J
Jacobites 96, 102, 108, 110, 112, 114,
    118, 128, 134
James I 64
James II 64
James III 28, 64
James IV 64, 68, 70, 72, 74, 146, 172
James V 70, 72, 74
James VI of Scotland, and I of
    England 32, 77, 82, 84, 86, 90, 102
James VII, and II of England 94,
    96, 102

James, 'the Old Pretender' 96, 108,
    110
Jardine, William 166
John Balliol 48, 50, 52, 72

K
Kenneth I (mac Alpin) 22, 24
Kenneth II 38
Kentigern, St 36
'Killing Time' 94
kilts 58, 114, 130, 132, 136
Knox, John 78, 80

L
Labour 184, 186, 188, 202, 208, 210–11
'lairds' 143
language 106
Large Hadron Collider 209
Largs, Battle of 26, 46
law and order 178
Lewis, Isle of 10
Liberals 182, 186
Lion Rampant 42
Lipton, Thomas 166
Lister, Joseph 150
literature 176
livestock 143–4
Loch Lomond 128, 194
Loch Ness 194
Lords of the Isles 68, 98
Lowlanders 112, 130, 132, 134, 143
Lowlands 5, 14, 30, 76, 98–9, 106,
    138, 158, 187

M
Mac Bethad mac Findlaich 32
McAdam, John Loudon 156

Macdonald, John A. 164, 184
MacDonald, Ramsey 184, 186
MacDonald Clan 68, 99
MacGregor, Rob Roy 128
Macleod, JJR 192
Macpherson, James 128
Macquarie, Lachlan 165
Maes Howe burial 10
Malcolm I 38
Malcolm III 32–4, 38, 40
Margaret, Maid 44, 48, 74
Margaret, St 33, 34, 40
Margaret Tudor 70, 74
Mary II 94, 96, 102
Mary of Guise 72, 74, 76
Mary, Queen of Scots 4, 72, 74, 77, 82, 88, 172
Matheson, James 166
Maxwell, James Clerk 152
medicine 150, 192
merchants 140, 166
Monymusk Reliquary 20

N

Napier, John 168
national anthem 56
National Covenant 86
national identity 6, 18, 214
nationalism 202
Neolithic peoples 10
New Lanark 142
Ninian, St 16
Normans 38, 40, 52, 62, 99
Northern Ireland 84
Northern Isles 4, 28
Norway 26, 44, 46, 68
Nova Scotia 116

O

Ogilvy, James 214–5
oil, North Sea 200
Orkney 26, 28
Ossian poems 128
Owen, Robert 142

P

Patrick, St 16
penicillin 154, 192
Perth 55, 64, 90, 165
Picts 4, 12, 18, 20, 22, 30
place names 30
prehistory 10
Presbyterianism 80, 86, 88, 92, 94, 98, 102
prime ministers 184
Protestantism 76–7, 80, 82, 84, 94, 96, 98, 102

R

radio 190
railways 156, 158, 164
referendum, 2014 211
Reformation 76, 78, 98
Reith, John 190
Robert I (the Bruce) 4, 52, 54, 58, 62
Robert II 62
Romans 4, 11, 12
Roslin 209
'Rough Wooing' 74
royal burghs 40
Royal Deeside 144
Royal Mile 78
Royal Navy 187, 196

S

St Andrews 60, 90, 172, 204
St Andrews Cathedral 60, 76
St Giles Cathedral 78, 90
saints 16, 18, 20, 28, 33, 36
Salmond, Alex 211
Saltire 18, 42, 84
Scone 24, 52, 92
Scots 5, 14, 20, 22, 30
Scots language 106, 176
'Scots Wha Hae' 56
Scott, Walter 128, 130, 132
Scottish National Party 188, 202, 211
Scottish Parliament 78, 88, 90, 92, 94, 98, 100, 102, 104, 122, 202, 208, 210, 214–5
Scottish regiments 114, 132, 134, 136
Scotus, John Duns 60
Second World War 196
Shakespeare, William 32
Shetland 26, 28, 200
shipbuilding 160
Simpson, James 150
Skara Brae, Orkney 10
Smith, Adam 118, 121
sport 172, 174, 180, 204
steam engines 138, 154, 160
Stevenson, Robert Louis 176
Stewart, Henry, Lord Darnley 77
Stewarts/Stuarts 55, 62, 64, 66, 74, 78, 88, 92, 96, 98, 102
Stirling 54–5, 90, 206
Stirling Bridge, Battle of 50, 55
Stirling Castle 52, 55
Stone of Destiny 24, 50
Stuart, Charles Edward 110, 112

Sturgeon, Nicola 211
succession 22, 102

T

tartan 130, 132, 136, 206
Tartan Day 58
telephones 154, 170
television 154, 190
textiles 142
thistle, the 46
trade 140, 166

U

Union of the Crowns, 1603 5, 82, 90, 92, 106
United States 116, 162
universities 60
urbanization 158, 182

V

Victoria, Queen 144
Vikings 26, 28, 30

W

Wallace, William 4, 50, 52
Watt, James 138, 154
whisky 146, 148
Whithorn 16
William I (the Lion) 40, 42, 64
William III (of Orange) 94, 102
Wilson, James 116
Witherspoon, John 116

Y

York, Treaty of 40
Young, James 158, 200

Picture Credits

Collins

LITTLE BOOKS

These beautifully presented Little Books make excellent pocket-sized guides, packed with hints and tips.

Bananagrams Secrets
978-0-00-825046-1
£6.99

Bridge Secrets
978-0-00-825047-8
£6.99

101 ways to win at Scrabble
978-0-00-758914-2
£6.99

Gin
978-0-00-825810-8
£6.99

HarperCollins

P U B L I S H E R S

Since 1817